Real Chocolate

Real Chocolate

Sweet and Savory Recipes for Nature's
Purest Form of Bliss

Chantal Coady

RIZZOLI
NEW YORK

I would like to dedicate this book to my children, Fergus and Millie, and their cousins, Cesar, Charlie, Emily, Frances, Jamie, JoJo, Laura, Maddie, Miranda, Nick, Peter, and Toby, and my godchildren, Jessica, Camila, and Theodora.

Editor & project manager: Lewis Esson
Design, art direction, & styling: Françoise Dietrich
Production: Tracy Hart
Illustrations: Chantal Coady
Photography: Richard Foster
(except for the photograph of the author on page 19, which is by Cindy Palmano for *The Face* magazine)
Home economist: Jane Suthering assisted by Thom Hughes

THROUGHOUT THE BOOK, WHENEVER RECIPES CALL FOR "REAL CHOCOLATE" WHAT IS MEANT IS BEST-QUALITY BITTERSWEET CHOCOLATE WITH MINIMUM 60 PERCENT COCOA LIQUOR, E.G., VALRHONA OR CALLEBAUT.
SOME RECIPES SPECIFY ITALIAN 00 (DOPPIO ZERO) FLOUR, AS USED IN MAKING FRESH PASTA AND AVAILABLE FROM ITALIAN AND SPECIALTY FOOD STORES. IF UNAVAILABLE, USE ANY FINE FLOUR OR ALL-PURPOSE.

First published in the United States of America in 2003
by Rizzoli International Publications, Inc.
300 Park Avenue South
New York, NY 10010

First published in the UK in 2003 by
Quadrille Publishing Limited,
Alhambra House, 27-31 Charing Cross Road,
London WC2H OLS

ISBN: 0-8478-2515-9

Printed in Germany

Library of Congress Control Number: 2002112218

contents

introduction

Almost twenty years have gone by since I first opened Rococo, my specialty chocolate store in London, and things have come a long way. I still love chocolate with a passion, and I am so happy to have been able to carve out my own niche in this extraordinary business, which continues to give so much pleasure to so many people. I really enjoy the opportunity to experiment with flavors and types of chocolate in a constantly evolving creative process. My hope is that this book will allow you to share some of that enjoyment.

Chantal Coady

London September 2002

chocolate facts

As I became more serious about chocolate issues, and I started to ask questions about the established order of the chocolate business, I opened a can of worms. I felt I had to offer a choice about the kind of chocolate people consumed and to give them the information they needed to make their choices. It is not that I want to dictate the kind of chocolate that is eaten, but I believe everyone should at least be able to taste the real thing and decide for themselves. In 1986, I started the Campaign for Real Chocolate to counter the multinational chocolate-makers argument that the addition of vegetable and other fats in chocolate is acceptable. At that time the European Union was trying to have this type of chocolate confectionery renamed "vegelate," which I found an apt description of the low-grade product masquerading as something else. The long-running battle was finally resolved with a fudge: The kind of candy bar that can be sold in the European market as "Family Milk Chocolate" contains primarily sugar and fat, with a lot of milk and not very much cocoa or cocoa butter. My campaign has been trying to establish the minimum acceptable level of cocoa, that cocoa butter is the only legitimate fat in a chocolate bar, and that sugar shouldn't be the primary ingredient.

In 1990, the campaign's aims were refocused with the launch of The Chocolate Society, which I founded with Nicola Porter. The message about Real Chocolate was widely trumpeted by the British press, and at last it seemed to gain support. A groundswell revolt against the low-standard, sugar- and fat-laden British chocolate started, and consumers began to read ingredients labels before purchasing a bar of chocolate. I suppose it is inevitable that sometimes only part of the message gets through, and it seems this is why the percentage of the cocoa content has become a deciding factor for many consumers. Of course, it is one determining factor, but only one, and the origin and quality of the beans are even more important. I have tasted many bars of chocolate with a high cocoa content, which have been very filthy tasting, with burned aromas and all sorts of other bad "notes." I hope this section of my book gives you all the information you need to make your own informed judgments on chocolate.

the history of chocolate

There are certain moments in the history of mankind when quantum leaps are made, such as when nomadic stone-age men settled long enough in one place to plant crops and domesticate animals; the invention of the wheel is another such moment, as was the discovery that the addition of lime to cornmeal, when soaked in water overnight, softened the tough outer husk of the cereal to make a protein-rich dough. The word for this process is nixtamalization, which comes from the language of Central American Olmecs, whose diet was transformed by the process. The Olmec people settled the fertile lowlands of the Gulf of Mexico, cultivating corn, chilies, avocados, pumpkins, and beans. And it was almost certainly the Olmecs who first cultivated the cocoa tree (*Theobroma cacao*).

The Olmec civilization lasted from around 500 B.C. to 1150 A.D., declining and eventually vanishing. The secret of nixtamalization was passed on to the Mayas, Toltecs, and Aztecs. The Spanish did not seem to understand or adopt it. They took corn to Europe, but, in spite of heavy grinding in mills to soften the grains, diseases caused by protein deficiencies such as pellagra were widespread among populations for many years. By the time Spanish explorer Hernán Cortés arrived with his conquistadors in "New Spain," the then dominant Aztecs were a stratified society with huge populations living in an organized and democratic order, including an established infrastructure of merchants, who distributed produce to markets all around the country. The Mayas, living as slaves, were banished to the Yucatán, where they grew the most important Aztec commodity—cacao. Cacao was made into a cold, spicy gruel that was an integral part of all rituals and ceremonies.

chocolate in europe

Hernán Cortés can take the credit for successfully taking cocoa to Europe. He could see its importance as a cash crop, because in Mexico the cocoa bean had a monetary value and was used in the place of small coins. Cortés had been searching for the gold of El Dorado, but he quickly realized that cocoa was a renewable source of "money." He took the beans and planted them in Haiti, Trinidad, and, it is believed, on the island of São Tomé. From there they were taken to the Ivory Coast, where much of the world's bulk cocoa is grown today. It was Cortés, too, who adapted the Aztec recipe for preparing chocolate gruel, so that the cold, fatty, and spicy drink, which some chroniclers called "a wash fitter for hogs," became a hot drink, with the addition of sugar, vanilla, and cinnamon. It appealed greatly to the European palate.

From cocoa's introduction to the royal court in Spain in the sixteenth century, it remained a closely guarded secret for a century. Then through a series of strategic royal marriages made to secure the future of the Holy Roman (later to become the Austro-Hungarian) empire, the drinking of chocolate spread through the palaces of Europe. At first it was drunk only in the privacy of the bedchamber, at breakfast time. Some critics were alarmed at the power of this beverage, which was said to be intoxicating. It was, in fact, the first alkaloid to be introduced into Europe, before tea and coffee.

During the seventeenth and eighteenth centuries chocolate remained the preserve of royalty and the aristocracy, because it was a highly taxed commodity. At this time cocoa was sold under special license by royal apothecaries, who regarded it more as a medicine than a foodstuff. Cocoa has always been a precious commodity, so, naturally, whenever there is money to be made, there will be a huckster trying to make a fast buck, and cocoa is no exception to this rule. There are accounts of Aztec cocoa beans being hollowed out and filled with earth, then passed off as counterfeit money. In Europe, brick dust was commonly found in the cocoa being sold by the less scrupulous merchants, and today the practice of adulteration continues in more insidious ways.

Cocoa was also an important commodity in the slave triangle. Ships would set sail from Liverpool and Bristol, in England, laden with ironware and textiles produced by the mills of the industrial Revolution, and exchange them with West African chiefs for a cargo of slaves. This human cargo was transported to the West Indies, where the slaves labored on sugar and cocoa plantations. A cargo of tropical hardwood, such as mahogany, or sugar, rum, and cocoa were loaded onto the ships for the last leg of the trip, back to England. There is an early account of pirates who, having seized a ship, jettisoned its cargo of cocoa beans believing them to be sheep droppings.

It was not until the middle of the nineteenth century (1852 in England) that taxation was slashed from 10 percent (two out of the twenty shillings in every pound sterling) to one penny per pound in weight of cocoa. It was also around this time that the revolution in the manufacture of cocoa came about. The Dutchman Coenraad Van Houten patented the cocoa press and the process of alkalizing cocoa, both of which removed the excess fatty components of cocoa to make it much more readily soluble as a drink. Then came the Swiss Rudolf Lindt, who invented the conch (see page 17) and "eating chocolate," as we know it today. At this stage, the big boys known so well today came on the scene: the Cadburys, the Frys, and the Rowntrees in England; Nestlé in Switzerland; Hershey and Bakers in the United States; following in the footsteps of Van Houten and Lindt. Many of the early industrial producers of chocolate were Quakers, who, being barred from the professions they might have followed, became industrialists. The Cadburys and Milton

Hershey built model villages for their workforces, educated the workers' children, and provided health care and near-Utopian conditions for the time. Chocolate was also heralded as a pure and healthy alternative to the dreaded gin, which had ruined the lives of so many working people before them. Chocolate was even marketed as "flesh forming," which, at the time, was as powerful a marketing tool as "low-fat" is today.

chocolate in the twentieth century

Ironically, it was those noble Quaker ideals that laid the foundations of our now degraded industrial food production. The world most of us inhabit has too much food, largely of dubious quality. Although there is no intrinsic reason why large-scale production should necessarily mean poor-quality products, it invariably does. Profit margins are the driving forces of these industries, and any small tweak in manufacturing process can result in a huge increase of the bottom line.

Probably the blackest day in chocolate history came in World War II when Milton Hershey invented a special nonmelting chocolate to send to American troops in the Far East, in their ration packs. The innovation involved removing the cocoa butter and replacing it with a waxy compound with a much higher melting point. The result was seized upon by chocolate manufacturers in Europe, particularly in England, Ireland, and Denmark, and has stuck in the throats of chocolate lovers ever since. For many people this is the norm, apart from being the only chocolate they've ever experienced, but a far cry from the real thing! On a happier note, in many parts of Europe the tradition of artisan food production has remained unaffected by the Industrial Revolution, particularly for chocolate-making. Although many of these traditions are under threat, there are also as many supporters. There are hundreds of small chocolate makers in France, as well as in Spain, Italy, Austria, Germany, Belgium, and Holland.

But to return to the history of chocolate. I now realize it is littered with inaccuracies that have been passed from one generation to the next in an unintentional game of telephone. Each writer, trusting unquestioningly material they have gleaned from respected treatises. I am not the first writer to have fallen into this trap, and, indeed, in my first book I, too, declared that the Aztecs used cinnamon to flavor their chocolate. The Spanish might have introduced them to this spice, but there is no evidence of trade between the Spice Islands in the East Indies and the Aztecs or Mayans. I am going to gloss over much of the early history of chocolate because there is finally a book, the definitive chocolate bible, *The True History of Chocolate* by Sophie and Michael Coe (Thames & Hudson, London 1996), which says it all. Unlike the other histories, this one has gone back to the original sources, so there is no danger of received fiction in this book—read it!

chocolate from bean to bar

Children brought up in Western consumer societies are so far removed from the reality of food production they can be forgiven for believing milk starts its life in a carton and has nothing to do with cows. In its own way, chocolate is another foodstuff with origins that are shrouded in mystery. We'll never know who first decided to eat this fruit, or who transformed it into cacao or cocoa, but I will try to demystify the process that transforms it into slabs of eating chocolate.

beginning with the bean

Cocoa trees grow in a very narrow belt ten to twenty degrees each side of the equator. They are fragile and need constant rainfall, warmth, and shelter from the wind and sun. Basically, there are two genetic types of cocoa—forastero and criollo. Forastero is the bulk cocoa grown for the commodity markets. With round pods, it is a high-yielding, hardy variety, the flavor of which is not considered to be particularly fine. Criollo is the original fine cocoa bean, a fragile—and now an endangered—species. The pods are red and elongated, and the flavor very fruity, redolent of raspberries, red currants, and citrus fruit. At present this bean accounts for less than 5 percent of world cocoa production.

Said to have been the result of natural cross-pollination after a hurricane in Trinidad in the eighteenth century, Trinitario is the name given to a hybrid cross of criollo and forastero. This variety is highly regarded by cocoa experts, as it has an excellent flavor with predominant green notes: apple, melon, oak, and balsam. There are many other hybrid beans, the best of which are fine in flavor and more robust than the criollo.

It might be helpful to think of cocoa beans in the same terms as coffee. At the extreme ends of the coffee scale, arabica and robusta beans. Arabica (equivalent to criollo) is regarded as the best, and it would be criminal to roast the beans black and hide their delicate flavour. Robusta coffee beans (equivalent to forastero), however, are almost always highly roasted and used to make very strong espresso coffee. Most of the hybrid cocoa beans fall into the category of "fine and flavor" beans, for which a premium is paid and due care is taken with their roasting, and so on.

transforming the cocoa bean into a commodity

Cocoa is often grown alongside shade trees, referred to as "mothers," such as coconut, banana, or plantain. The ripe cocoa pods, which come in many shapes, sizes, and colors (generally looking like footballs up to one foot long), are harvested with great care. A machete is used to cut the pod from the tree trunk and it must be cleaned after each cut, to prevent disease being spread in the humid growing conditions on the plantations. The pod is slashed open and the many small, white fruits piled on a mat of plantain leaves. The mound of beans is then covered with more leaves and left to ferment for seven days. Soft white flesh, which tastes a little like rambutan or mangosteen, surrounds the glossy dark seed, which is, in fact, the cocoa bean. The sweet flesh provides the sugar for the natural fermentation process during which the beans develop their characteristic chocolatey flavor. The residue of the fruit evaporates and leaves behind traces of acetic acid.

The beans are then dried in the sun. This part of the process can be problematic, because cocoa is grown in the rain forest, so daily downpours are the norm. Some growers have roll-on covers, a bit like the ones used to cover tennis courts; others resort to oven-drying, which is not usually the solution as beans dried in this way are often tainted with smoke, which annihilates the fine flavor of the cocoa beans. Dried beans are graded and sorted, and put into sacks to be transported to the enduser. Good cocoa buyers will take a sample of about 100 beans from each sack and count how many bad beans are found. Beans are rejected if they are moldy or have started to sprout. The remaining good beans are then shipped to chocolate factories all around the world, where they will be transformed into the dark and delicious chocolate bars we love so much.

the chocolate-making process

At the factory, the beans are checked for quality before being roasted. Roasting is a great skill; the beans need to be roasted at a temperature of 250 to 285 degrees, to result in a wonderful, intense flavor. The art is in making sure that the beans are roasted long enough to bring out the flavor, while being careful not to burn them. The next process is known as winnowing, similar to separating wheat from chaff. The outer layer of the cocoa bean is blown away (and collected to become mulch for gardens); the inner seed will be transformed into chocolate.

What sort of chocolate the beans are destined to become determines the next stage. "Fast chocolate" will be made quickly (in about twelve hours), and often the cocoa butter will be removed and replaced with other fats, as well as other artificial additives. "Slow chocolate" will be milled through a series of heavy metal rollers, and then refined farther in conches, which pummel it between granite rollers at a temperature of 126 to 186 degrees for up to a week. (The conch, named after the shell, was invented by Rodolfe Lindt in 1880.) The longer chocolate is conched, the smaller the particle size. The finest chocolate will have particles measuring eighteen to twenty microns, so small as to be indiscernible to the palate. Also, the more slowly the chocolate is refined, the more acetic acid will evaporate and the mellower the chocolate will become.

and what is added in the process?

The finest chocolate will have extra cocoa butter added to make the chocolate even smoother and quicker to melt in the mouth. Normally, sugar is added to the chocolate–the quantity depends on the type of chocolate. Good dark chocolate will have around 30 percent sugar, while fast chocolate may have up to 80 percent.

Milk chocolate will have milk added, in the form of milk "crumb" or condensed milk. The milk crumb gives a slightly cheesy or farmyard flavor to the chocolate. American and British chocolate are made with crumb, whereas Swiss and other European chocolate is made from condensed milk (invented by Henri Nestlé), which gives a much smoother, creamier texture. White chocolate is made from cocoa butter, milk, and sugar, but does not contain any dry cocoa matter.

Cocoa-butter substitutes are used widely in fast chocolates. These are made from hydrogenated vegetable fats, such as palm, rape, or soya oil, or karite or mahua (illipe) butter, all of which are less expensive than cocoa butter. The effect of hydrogenation is to turn oils into solid fats by changing their molecular structure. In the process, normally quite healthy fatty acids are changed into trans-fatty acids, which can inhibit the body's ability to absorb good fatty acids. They are sometimes called "fractionated oils" on labels, to disguise them.

These fats also have a higher melting point than cocoa butter, which helps to stabilize the chocolate in warm conditions. In my opinion, there can never be any justification for the addition of these fats to replace cocoa butter. Noncocoa-butter fats do not melt at blood temperature, and these solid particles leave a greasy residue that sticks to the palate, the effect of which is cloying.

Cocoa butter is a unique fat. It is saturated and yet behaves like an unsaturated fat. It contains oleic acid and, like olive oil, has been shown to reduce blood cholesterol levels. It also melts at just below blood temperature, as you will know if you have ever held chocolate in your hand. The melting point is one of the most remarkable things about cocoa butter, as it melts on the tongue, it feels cool, it transforms the chocolate into a liquid which penetrates the taste buds and releases the volatile aromas up into the nose.

the genesis of Rococo

"Whatever made you think of opening a chocolate store?" I have lost count of the number of people who've asked me that. To me the answer is so obvious I am amazed that anyone need ask. I have always been obsessed by chocolate, as far back as I can remember, and I thought everyone dreamed of opening their own chocolate store. Perhaps they did when they were small, but then forgot about it or got sensible and decided to follow conventional careers. My dream was recurrent, and many a time I walked through landscapes from *Charlie and the Chocolate Factory*, where the trees were swathed in candies, blades of grass made from soft minty sugar, and rivers filled with molten chocolate. Each time I picked the candies, gathered them in my skirts, and returned home to hide them under my pillow, so they would be there when I woke. So vivid were these dreams . . . . so bitter the disappointment on waking and finding nothing.

I suppose in a way I deviated from my childhood fantasy when I went to art school, but it was there that I was given my dream ticket to chocolate heaven, or so I thought. I was offered a vacation job in the confectionery department of Harrods, at that time the archetypal British department store, statted mainly by veterans who had worked there at least forty years. My immediate superior was a vodka-soaked tyrant who refused to give shopping bags to the day-trippers buying Mars bars. In spite of having a wonderful array of the finest chocolates available at that time, the atmosphere in the department was funereal, and the customers were largely treated with contempt. No one I worked with seemed to realize that they were purveying probably the finest handmade chocolates available in London. To me the chocolates were a revelation to behold and taste, and everyone I gave them to (I had a generous staff discount) was in raptures. Surely I was not alone in understanding that this chocolate had the power to transport the most hardened individual.

Everyone thought I was crazy when I said I was going to open my own chocolate store. I thought there was a niche for something completely different–more along the lines of a French *boutique de chocolat*–which would allow the customer to indulge in his wildest chocolate dreams, and no one succeeded in talking me out of it. I did a ten-week Start Your Own Business course and was twenty-three when my student bank manager agreed to lend me the start-up money. He wanted his pound of flesh in return, and, as I was penniless, my dear mother gave it by securing the loan with her house. Was this an act of supreme indulgence on her part, or did she believe I had inherited the female entrepreneurial streak from her side of the family (her mother and

grandmother had both owned stores)? For my part, business failure was just not a possibility, due
to a mixture of blind faith and youthful *chutzpah*.

the dream becomes reality

I found a store in the King's Road, which I felt was the perfect location. The type of shopper on
the street was very mixed: Punks extorting money from Japanese tourists who took their
photographs; the privileged Chelsea children (who bought, sold, and consumed serious drugs in
the local hostelries); and the residents who were to become the hard core of my clientele. Having
vowed never to sell rose or violet creams, I had to buck up my ideas fast if I was going to keep
the establishment happy. I managed to persuade small family chocolate makers to supply me
with a range of handmade chocolate and Easter eggs, and also found suppliers of sugared
almonds and other delicacies at the huge trade fair in Cologne. I certainly had no idea about how
to actually make chocolates at that time, but I did have an idea about what was good, even if my
attitude to customer services was somewhat remiss.

Opening the store three weeks before Easter nearly killed me. However, with the help of many
kind people, including suppliers, who probably thought I was mad or a rich kid on a whim, I
somehow managed to pull it all together. To begin with I ran the store with
the help of my brother and sister, but we spent as much time
bickering as serving customers, so after a while they went
their separate ways. I had one salutary experience in

the first month of opening when I was quoted in the business section of *The Sunday Times.* My response to the question, "What is the worst thing about running you own business?," was, "You could say we get a fair number of insufferable old bags in here." I was definitely in post-Harrods trauma, and, fortunately, only one young man took me to task over it, saying, "You might have been talking about *my* mother!"

Luckily, few of the people who did read the piece ever identified themselves as being old bags, and most seemed amused by the *faux pas*. Soon I was a reformed character, and when someone was particularly rude or obnoxious, I would smile extra sweetly, never rise to the bait, and gradually there would be a sea change. My favorite old lady, Miss Biddy Cook, one of the fiercest old bags, even apologized for her early behavior when she had taken every opportunity to get under my skin and failed miserably. It made my day when she said, "My Dear, I am so ashamed about how I used to behave when you first opened. I really did not believe that you stood a chance. . . ."

With the help of my art-school friends, Frank Taylor and Kitty Arden, I transformed the interior of the shop into a theatrical stage set inspired by the word *rococo*. The walls were stippled in candy-floss pink, and so was my hair. I found the only person in England who could make a chandelier out of sugar, and I gradually transformed myself into an eighteenth-century stage character, with punk overtones. This all sounds rather ridiculous now, but at the time it seemed the right thing to do and everyone seemed to love it. What was right, though, was my feeling that most people could share my passion for real chocolate, and that by following this conviction I was capable of changing the perception of chocolate for countless individuals.

The word *rococo* started to have deeper resonance for me and the business as I discovered that there was a rococo period in London, and much of it based around the area in which I lived and worked: There were the Chelsea Potters, who made exquisite platters covered in shells and crustacea; the Ranelagh and Vauxhall Pleasure Gardens, where Handel performed his operas; and the Huguenot silk weavers, who took refuge in Spitalfields, away from the political persecution in France. I played only baroque music or opera in the store, and became something of a "barocky." I was thereby able to add a musical dimension to the Rococo experience.

the inspiration of eurochocolate
In 1994, I was asked to write a guide to the world's best chocolate makers. This was a pretty tall order, especially as the publisher did not even have a database of chocolate makers, and I had

only weeks to do the research, taste the chocolates, and write the book. It was a wonderful challenge, and with the help of the Comitato del Cioccolato, who were launching "Eurochocolate" for the first time, I met many small and medium-size chocolate makers who had been brought together in Perugia, Italy. The difference between this event and the many other chocolate-themed occasions that I have attended over the years was that it was driven by real passion, not commercial gain.

Started by Eugenio Guarducci, a maverick architect-cum-hotelier, everyone was thrown together in a chaotic maelstrom. I made many firm friends that year and have returned every year since, although, sadly, the event has now been hijacked by the Perugia City Council, who see it as a gravy train to bring in thousands of visitors from all over Italy. The Corso Vannucci, a huge medieval boulevard, was so full last year, I could picture a public execution, only here the crowds gathered around the scaffolds were baying for chocolate, not blood. The other thing that surprised and delighted me was the generosity of spirit with which all the chocolate makers shared their recipes and secret tips. In some ways it is like giving a musician a score—each one will produce a different rendering of the piece, depending on the musical instrument or raw material, the degree of virtuosity, and the emotion that goes into the performance. The recipes themselves are merely the starting point.

rococo today

I was so inspired by what I witnessed in Italy in 1994 that I decided it was time for Rococo to get serious and start producing as much as possible in house. I had a little knowledge about the technical side of chocolate making, but could see that many of the best chocolate makers were, in fact, trained in a completely different discipline, and were self-taught.

I gave a very basic training to Joanna Gaskell, my new chocolate maker, who pretty quickly knew much more than I did about tempering chocolate and making truffles. We built a tiny chocolate kitchen in my house, and soon we needed another chocolate maker. Today, Ruth Morgan, who originally trained as a sculptor and designer, has joined Jo.

The kitchen is really too small now and we are considering a new space. There we will be able to produce a larger range of chocolate, but still all made by hand. Rococo has jumped through the necessary hoops to get organic certification on the artisan bars, made using really fine organic chocolate and different herbs and spices, combined to achieve balance and flavor.

the truth about real chocolate

Real chocolate and fast chocolate are very distant relations. I use the word *fast* to differentiate the kind of industrial low-grade chocolate readily available and normally consumed as fast food.

real chocolate is actively good for you

Among the purposes of this book is to give real chocolate a positive image and to let everyone feel good about eating and enjoying it. It is one of the most nutritious and easily digested foods known to man. It contains a multitude of vitamins (A1, B1, B2, C, D, and E), minerals (calcium, potassium, sodium, magnesium, iron, zinc, copper, chromium, and phosphorous), and complex alkaloids, all of which enhance health and well-being. The iron in chocolate also comes in a form 93 percent useable by the body; the oxalic acid present helps bond the iron and calcium so it is bioavailable.

Real chocolate is low in sugar and has a low glycemic index, meaning it keeps you feeling full for longer and helps keep your blood glucose levels steady. The glycemic index of chocolate is forty-nine (forty-five for milk chocolate), and anything under 50 is considered low: Potato chips, cookies, white bread, and other refined carbohydrates have a high glycemic index. There is strong evidence that replacing desserts with good chocolate can help weight loss and diabetes. (See *A Chocolate a Day Keeps the Doctor Away* by Dr. John Ashton and Suzy Ashton, Souvenir Press, London, 2002.)

There is a naturally occurring antidepressant in chocolate called phenylethylamine (PEA) which increases the serotonin levels in the brain. They can induce a euphoric state, as well as boosting energy levels and mental alertness. High PEAs are found in "love-addicted" women; low PEA levels are found in people who are depressed. Chocolate affects the hormones in the brain in a similar way to morphine, and so can relieve pain. Prozac is the man-made chemical used to treat depression by raising serotonin levels; it also has many well-documented side effects and is highly addictive. Real chocolate, however, acts as an instant antidepressant. Even its smell can have a calming effect on the brain. Chocolate also contains theobromine and valeric acid. The former is a stimulant similar to caffeine, with a chemical composition that is only one atom different, but is weaker in its action. It stimulates the brain, muscles, and central nervous system, and has also been shown to lower blood pressure.

Chocolate is also rich in flavinoids (also found in red wine) and other chemical compounds known to reduce the likelihood of deep-vein thrombosis and strokes. Although red wine is excellent in moderate amounts, alcohol can be dangerous, but I have never heard of anyone being killed by eating real chocolate. Cocoa butter has been proven to lower blood cholesterol levels, and chocolate is rich in antioxidants, which help to destroy the unhealthy free radicals and boost the immune system, two of the most important factors in preventing cancer.

Chocolate is even used as a homeopathic remedy, indicated for feelings of hostility, especially when mothers feel anger and frustration toward their offspring. The effect is to restore the nurturing mother side and to promote a general sense of well-being. (Interestingly, one theory why we love chocolate so much from an early age is that, in many respects, white chocolate is the closest thing to human breast milk.) The other surprising finding is that cocoa possesses antibacterial properties, which help to prevent tooth decay. It seems most dentists agree that even chocolate containing sugar is significantly less harmful than candies, such as lollipops, in relation to dental caries.

fast chocolate

Fast chocolate contains as little as 5 percent cocoa, while the other ingredients are usually sugar, solid hydrogenated vegetable fats, nut oils, and a host of artificial flavorings. These types of fats are hidden in so many processed foods, and it is difficult to imagine that this kind of chocolate can possibly make a positive contribution to your health. The use of any fat other than cocoa butter is to my mind unacceptable. Cocoa butter occurs naturally in cocoa beans, and it has many qualities that make it a desirable commodity in its own right. The cosmetics and pharmaceutical industries buy tons of the stuff every year, to make into lipsticks, creams, and suppositories, for which they are happy to pay a premium. It must be sorely tempting for industrial chocolate makers to remove the cocoa butter and sell it on, substituting other cheap and readily available hydrogenated fats. You might ask, "What difference does it make anyway?" Firstly, you can feel the difference in the mouth—these trans fats do not melt properly and leave a greasy coating on the palate. More importantly, perhaps, some hydrogenated fats have been linked with serious health problems, whereas cocoa butter acts to lower blood-cholesterol levels.

looking for the real thing

Real chocolate can be hunted out easily enough—it is mostly a question of learning to read and interpret the wrappers. Look out for high cocoa content, but there's no need to exaggerate; 50 to 70 percent cocoa solids are usually a good sign. I don't know anyone who drinks wine who would select a bottle using the alcohol content as a guide to quality. Normally the deciding factors would be the grape variety, appellation, vintage year, country of origin, as well as the color.
A reliable indicator in recognizing real chocolate is the use of natural vanilla rather than vanillin, an

artificial flavoring derived from pine trees. It is not that I am so against vanillin in itself, but it does seem to be a good marker to differentiate the sheep from the goats. The price of vanillin is almost negligible and, hence, it is used injudiciously, often with a view to masking the true nature of the cocoa beans in an inferior product. In spite of this general rule, there are plenty of examples of excellent chocolate containing vanillin. Probably the best way of spotting a really fine chocolate is to find out about the origin and variety of the cocoa beans.

I have often heard people say, "I don't like dark chocolate—it's bitter." There are very few who, having tasted the real thing, still protest. The reality is that low-quality chocolate is often bitter, in spite of the high sugar content. This is because the cocoa beans used have been overroasted and then they are padded out with sugar and (usually hydrogenated) fat to compensate for their poor flavor. Real chocolate makers select their cocoa beans very carefully; indeed, the similarity to wine making or coffee roasting comes to mind. Fine-flavored varieties of beans are carefully roasted to enhance the flavor. The process of refining the chocolate is a slow one, and extra cocoa butter is usually added to give the most sensuous, silken texture when melting in the mouth.

I don't wish to dwell on the negative aspects of fast chocolate, but it is essential that you are able to differentiate between that and real chocolate. This understanding might help wean you off the sugar high so commonly induced by the inferior confectionery. Once you have been initiated to the joys of really satisfying chocolate that hits the spot, the temptation to eat the fast chocolate might just evaporate. Good chocolate contains 512 calories per 3½ ounces (100g), so ⅙ ounce (one square of thin good quality chocolate–the perfect amount I think) will have less than twenty-six calories. A small apple weighs 3½ ounces and has forty-six calories.

the five senses chocolate test

Now that you know the difference between real and fast chocolate, put your knowledge to the test with my Five Senses Chocolate Test. It's a fun thing to do and gets you thinking about chocolate as never before. Start with four or five bars of high-quality semisweet chocolate, selecting ones with a range of cocoa-solids content from 30 to 70 percent. Test the chocolate with 70 percent cocoa solids first, then move down the scale. You need to start with a clean palate, so drink some water. Too much sugar or salt interferes with the tasting, as do strong flavors like mint or chili.

smell

We all know how when we have a cold, food just seems to lose its flavor and everything tastes the same. That's because smell is without doubt the most finely tuned of all the five senses. So

the first thing to do is to sniff the chocolate and determine what you can smell. Some of the aromas will remind you of intense fruit, wood, tobacco, caramel, or even burned rubber. Like a good wine, a good chocolate will have a well-balanced, pleasing smell.

sight

Next, break the bar of chocolate. When it's snapped, you should see a very characteristic texture in the break, a bit like tree bark. The other things to look for are the condition and color of the chocolate: It should be glossy, without any "bloom." A bloom indicates the chocolate has been stored in damp or warm conditions. The color of the chocolate will tell you about the type of cocoa used, and how highly roasted it is. In general, the redder the hue, the better the cocoa.

touch

Real chocolate should melt when held in the hand for a few seconds. The reason for this is that cocoa butter is solid and crystalline at 92 degrees, but melts at 94 degrees. The speed of melting is an indicator of what proportion of cocoa butter the chocolate contains: The higher the proportion, the better quality the chocolate, and the faster it melts.

sound

Break the chocolate next to your ear. Real chocolate has a distinctive snap caused by the cocoa butter crystals. Fast chocolate is more like plasticine; expect a dull thud.

taste

At last you've reached the stage you've been waiting for. You might think that tasting the chocolate will give you the best idea of its quality, but your tongue will also tell you how smooth the chocolate is, or, in other words, the particle size. In real chocolate, this should be so fine that it will not be discernible. The taste test will also reveal the chocolate's finish. Real chocolate should linger deliciously in the mouth, like good wine. If there's any greasy residue, it means the chocolate contains fats other than cocoa butter. And finally, as the chocolate melts in the mouth, it releases volatile aromas . . . and we're back to smell again. Enjoy!

*chocolate
know-how*

master class: ganache

ganache

A ganache, otherwise known as a truffle, is one of the essential building blocks that will be used again and again in this book. Once mastered, it is simple and will revolutionize the way you cook with chocolate.

The basic ganache is an emulsion of chocolate, cream, and butter. Some recipes will omit the butter when the finished result might be overrich. You can also use custard instead of cream, as in the Pear and Chocolate Tart (page 130), for a lighter and healthier mixture. Sometimes you will use the "raw" ganache, which will set to a stiff truffle texture when chilled, and other times the ganache will be cooked, as in the tart.

makes 6 cups

2¼ cups whipping cream

18 ounces real dark chocolate

½ cup (1 stick) unsalted butter, diced

Always use the best chocolate you can. (See Looking for the Real Thing, page 23.) Chop it into chunks or break it into squares. In a food processor, continue to chop the chocolate until it is a fine powder: it might actually just start to melt, but that's fine. If you have any big lumps, it can spoil your ganache. Put the chocolate into a heatproof bowl.

Scald the cream in a pan, allowing it to boil and rise up (be careful it doesn't boil over). Pour about 1 tablespoon onto the chocolate and mix well. Keep adding the cream, a spoonful at a time, mixing it in thoroughly. This method should guarantee the perfect emulsion (the process is a bit like making mayonnaise).

When all the cream has been incorporated, add the butter. The mixture should still be warm enough to melt it, although it will take a few minutes to beat it in until there are no lumps left. Don't be tempted to use melted butter, because this makes a very heavy ganache.

water ganache

When I was initially told of a French *chocolatier* making water ganache, my first reaction was that this sounded impossible. The idea of a ganache is basically that of an emulsion of two fatty components, like egg yolks and oil when making mayonnaise. A ganache of water and chocolate breaks all the rules of chocolate-making. However, because water and chocolate are sworn enemies (see below), I liked the idea of this challenge and decided to try it. The result was astonishing—it worked, and was surprisingly "creamy," in spite of not containing any cream. It did not split and was eaten without hesitation by all my family. I use it for low-fat mousses and cakes. There is also a version with tea, and it can be made with coffee, too. Experiment and see what other ideas you can come up with.

makes 6 small cups

8 ounces real dark chocolate (pages 23–4)

1 cup boiling water

cream or crème fraîche, to serve

(optional)

Break or chop the chocolate into pieces and melt in a low oven. (See Melting Chocolate, below.) When melted, make the ganache by adding the boiling water to the chocolate, spoonful by spoonful. It will thicken quickly at first, but it should become a smooth mixture when all the water is incorporated. (See Ganache, page 30.) Divide among 6 small coffee cups or glasses and chill. Serve with cream or crème fraîche, if you want.

melting chocolate

I never use a bain-marie—or even the traditional improvised bowl over a pan of hot water—to melt chocolate, as there is a danger that steam will get into the chocolate and ruin it. Much simpler is to use a very low oven (100–200 degrees) and put the chopped chocolate in a heatproof bowl. Leave in the oven for 5 minutes, then check with a fork; leave for another minute if it isn't all melted and test again. In the old days many chocolate-makers used a box with a light bulb set under a bowl, and the chocolate was left to melt overnight.

tea ganache (vegan)

serves 6

8 ounces real dark chocolate

4 teaspoons fine perfumed tea like
   Earl Grey

1 cup boiling water

touch of orange-flower water (optional)

cream or crème fraîche, to serve
   (optional)

Break or chop the chocolate into pieces and melt in a low oven. (See Melting Chocolate, opposite.) After it is melted, make the tea in a teapot, using the boiling water: Let it stand 2 minutes, but it must not stew! Make the ganache, adding the tea to the chocolate, spoonful by spoonful. It will thicken quickly at first, but it should become a smooth mixture when all the tea is incorporated (See Ganache, page 30.) Stir in the orange-flower water, if using. Divide among 6 small teacups or glasses and chill a few hours. Serve with cream or crème fraîche, if you wish.

plain-and-simple chocolate sauce

This is an easy recipe, using roughly one part of water to two parts of chocolate by weight.

7 tablespoons water

7 ounces real dark chocolate, chopped

Boil the water in a heavy-bottomed saucepan, then add the chocolate to the boiling water, whisking all the time and being careful not to let it burn. The mixture should be a thick glossy, perfectly smooth sauce. Serve with vanilla ice cream or anything else you like.

variation

For a spicy chocolate sauce, stir in a pinch each of ground cardamom and chili.

plain chocolate truffles

There are many ways to skin a cat . . . With truffles, everyone has their own recipe and variations on the basic method: some whip the cream before adding it to the melted chocolate—I normally use very finely chopped chocolate that is melted by the boiling cream; some whisk the truffle mixture when it is finished to aerate it. I prefer a dense, intense mixture, but it's a very personal thing.

Here are a few variations from some famous chocolate makers. Frederic Bau from the producer Valrhona says the chopped-chocolate-and-boiled-cream method gives the longest-lasting flavor, which is only really a consideration if you want to make the truffles long in advance.

Rococo recipe

(makes about 100)
(as in basic Ganache recipe, page 30)

18 ounces real dark chocolate
2¼ cups whipping cream
½ cup (1 stick) unsalted butter
unsweetened cocoa powder, to dust

Robert Linxe's recipe

for La Maison du Chocolat
(makes about 75)
(the high priest of chocolatiers)

9 ounces Valrhona Caraque
9 ounces Valrhona extra-bitter chocolate
1¼ cups whipping cream
more chocolate, to enrobe
unsweetened cocoa powder, to dust

Michel Chaudun's recipe

(makes about 100)

1½ pounds real dark chocolate
1¼ cups whipping cream
¼ vanilla bean
3½ tablespoons butter, softened
2¼ cups unsweetened cocoa powder

Make a ganache with the cream and chocolate as described on page 30, infusing the vanilla (Michel Chaudun's recipe) in the cream as you warm it. Let cool in a bowl or tray about 15 minutes in the refrigerator, then beat in the butter (Rococo and Michel Chaudun recipes), and return to the refrigerator. When the ganache has set to the consistency of buttercream icing, it is ready to be piped or spooned into truffle-size pieces.

If piping, put the mixture into a pastry bag and pipe blobs of ganache about the size of a large cherry onto a tray lined with waxed paper or plastic wrap. Let cool at least 2 hours, preferably 24.

To finish, you may dip the truffles in tempered chocolate (described in detail on page 45), using a dipping fork or your fingers, then drop onto a large baking tray generously filled with unsweetened cocoa powder. Roll briefly and let set; shake off excess. (Don't worry, most of the cocoa powder can be reused.)

white chocolate, cardamom, and saffron truffles

This recipe is a Rococo classic. I have always loved saffron, and when it is married with cardamom it has a particular resonance for me. The other great thing is that cardamom takes the sometimes rather sickly-sweet edge off the white chocolate. If you don't like these flavors or would like to substitute another, feel free to experiment—try nutmeg or anything else you fancy.

makes about 100

18 ounces real white chocolate

about 15 cardamom pods

1½ cups whipping cream

1 teaspoon ground saffron

1 cup (2 sticks) unsalted butter, softened

Chop the white chocolate finely in a blender or food processor.

Remove the outer skin from cardamom pods and warm the seeds in small a pan, then crush them using a mortar and pestle.

Put the cream, saffron, and cardamom seeds in a saucepan and boil 2 minutes. Make a ganache with the chocolate and cream as described on page 30, adding the butter at the end. Pipe into blobs on a waxed-paper or plastic-wrap-lined plate or scoop into truffle shapes with a spoon; let cool at least 2 hours, preferably 24.

Dip the truffles in tempered chocolate (page 45), either white or dark. This can be tricky, as the white chocolate makes the mixture soft and prone to melting as the truffles are dipped, so do it quickly and with a light hand.

variation
Finish by rolling them in chopped pistachio nuts instead of dipping in chocolate.

master class: tempering, molding, and sculpting

tempering chocolate

Tempering (also known as precrystallization) is probably the most frustrating aspect of chocolate-making until you understand how it works. The principles are really very simple, and once mastered, tempering is a very straightforward procedure. It is a bit like learning to drive: It's the sort of thing that you have to do by yourself a few times until you master the technique. There is definitely a technique. The good news is that you can retemper chocolate over and over again, as long as you melt it correctly and it does not have a sugar or humidity bloom. (See Storing Chocolate on page 88.)

When I was showing a class of five-year-olds how tempering is done, I used the example of schoolchildren running around in the playground (melted chocolate, all the crystals elements dispersed), then, when the bell rings, all the children form into orderly lines (or perfect chains of cocoa butter crystals in tempered chocolate). Cocoa butter is intrinsically unstable and by tempering chocolate, you are stabilizing it.

the reasons for tempering chocolate are:

1) To give a beautiful gloss to molded chocolate.

2) To help the chocolate shrink away from a mold and unmold perfectly.

3) To give the desired hardness and crystalline texture and crisp snap when broken.

4) To give stability to chocolate and help its keeping properties.

5) To prevent blooming (page 88).

essential equipment:

1) As large a slab of marble as you can reasonably manage. The Rococo slab is about 1 yard by 2 yards, but a much smaller one will do. However, the larger the slab, the easier tempering is. At home, I have one small piece of marble that is 24 by 16 inches. Tempering on it is really a bit fiddly, but it is possible.

2) A digital thermometer, which can be bought from any serious cookware store and should not break the bank.

3) A large metal spatula.

4) A triangular spreading knife—a large plasterer's filling knife from a hardware store is as good as anything, but it must be flexible.

5) Several stainless-steel or Pyrex bowls.

let's get started!

1 Melt (decrystallize) as much chocolate as you need in a heatproof bowl until it is completely fluid, without any lumps. The temperature of the melted chocolate should be 136 to 142 degrees for semisweet or bittersweet chocolate, 116 to 126 degrees for milk and white chocolate.

2 Then pour three-quarters of the chocolate onto a cool, dry marble slab. When I say "cool," this means not warmed by bowls of chocolate, but not artificially cool: that would cause the chocolate to crystallize too quickly. If that happens it will develop a bloom and be difficult to work. Scrape chocolate remaining in the bowl down the sides, so it doesn't cool too quickly.

3 Using a paddle or scraper (see Essential Equipment, left), spread the chocolate over the marble. This cools down the mass of chocolate and starts to encourage the formation of the crystalline structure.

4 Holding the paddle in one hand and the spatula in the other, quickly regroup the chocolate into the center of the marble, being careful not to leave any trails behind, because they will cool too quickly: We are aiming to keep the temperature uniform as it cools. Repeat Steps 3 and 4 a few times—notice how the chocolate begins to thicken.

5 Use a digital thermometer to check the temperature, but don't waste time as the chocolate is cooling quickly. When the dark chocolate has dropped to 82 to 84 degrees (milk chocolate 78 to 82 degrees, white chocolate 78 to 80 degrees) it is tempered and ready for the remaining melted chocolate to be added. Be careful that it does not get too cool; you might be able to gently warm it, or you might have to start all over again! Many professional chocolatiers test the temperature by dipping their finger into the chocolate and then touching their bottom lip, because it is time-consuming checking the thermometer all the time. In fact, the lip is a very accurate gauge of temperature once you know what you are doing.

6 Now add the remaining one-quarter of melted chocolate. This will bring up the temperature by about 30 degrees, which is the final stage of the "tempering curve"

(melting, cooling, and then raising the temperature slightly). Perfectly tempered chocolate has a very fine satin sheen; a dull finish is a sign that the chocolate has cooled too much and was not properly tempered.

7 Now the chocolate is ready to mold or dip truffles in. You need to be quick, because the chocolate will lose its temper if it warms up or cools down. Transfer the tempered chocolate to a heatproof bowl. You can place the bowl of tempered chocolate in a bain-marie of lukewarm water (baby's bath temperature), which will help to keep it workable for longer.

Keep practicing—after about 10 attempts you should be pretty good!

tips

A marble slab or other cool flat surface is essential. Work from one end of the marble to the other, and then back again so that the temperature of the marble remains stable. At the end don't be tempted to scrape off the hard bits from your scraper and spatula, because this will mess up your tempered chocolate—leave for consumption later, or give them to any willing helpers to eat. A stable room temperature of 66 to 74 degrees helps, as does low humidity—less than 50 percent. Different chocolates have different tempering curves. The precise temperatures vary with each chocolate. This is a technical point, and most manufacturers supply this information to anyone who needs it, as it is important for good results.

For most real dark chocolate, the starting temperature of the melted chocolate should not exceed 142 degrees; for milk or white chocolate, 126 degrees is the upper limit, because of the casein, or milk protein, they contain. This protein is very sensitive to heat and will suddenly seize at 144 degrees, rendering the chocolate useless.

Couverture is the technical name for the best-quality cooking chocolat—not to be confused with artificial chocolate or chocolate-flavored products that do not deserve to be called chocolate. Couverture must contain at least 32 percent cocoa butter. This rich chocolate is very fluid in its molten state and easy to work with, yet it is very crisp and brittle when tempered.

chocolate curls or flakes or bark

Use 5 ounces warm tempered chocolate (say using excess left over after making the molded hearts or trees later) and spread on the marble slab with a metal scraper until the chocolate is about ⅛ inch thick and about 12x 9½ inches; let set a few minutes. You will get different results if the chocolate is set, but not too hard, or if it is still a bit soft; both are good—experiment. With the scraper, push the edge of the chocolate sheet firmly and evenly, at an angle of about 45 degrees. You might get chocolate cigars, or it might crumple into flakes. If it's a disaster, melt the chocolate and start again.

chocolate leaves

These are easy and fun for children and adults alike. Experiment with different leaves. Those I find work best are reasonably thick but still flexible. Bay and holly can be too stiff, and ivy and bamboo too flimsy. The surfaces of leaves varies too—some shiny, others flat. My favorites are hydrangea and camellia. Try a selection.

5 ounces tempered chocolate, warm
24 leaves (see above)

You can paint either side of the leaf, but I do undersides, as the veining comes out better. Paint carefully: the important thing, especially if children are involved, is to keep the other sides clean. If there is chocolate on the wrong side it can cause the chocolate leaves to break when you peel them off. When dry, paint on another layer, and repeat again if you have the patience. Let set about 20 minutes, then carefully peel real leaves from chocolate ones.

dipped fruit

When you have mastered the art of tempering, temper about 5 ounces
of chocolate of your choice. I find white chocolate and strawberries work
very well together, and dark chocolate is good with firmer fruits like
cherries and cape gooseberries.

Pick really perfect fruit and half-dip in the still-warm chocolate. Place the
fruit on waxed paper on a plate and refrigerate. You don't need to worry
about condensation, because these will not be hanging around! Eat as
soon as they are ready, about 10 minutes. You can also dip nuts and
candied peel—anything you want really.

choc-dipped truffles

To dip truffles, you need roughly the same amount of chocolate again as you used to
make the ganache, although when tempering chocolate it is always easier to temper a
large quantity and make a batch of different things, such as the leaves, hearts, and trees.
If you temper the chocolate used for dipping, the truffles will have a crisp shell that
contrasts with the soft ganache filling. (You can also roll the truffles in cocoa, confectioners' sugar, coconut, chopped nuts, or anything else you wish.)

If you want truffles to last as long as possible, leave the dipping till 24 to 48 hours after
you make and shaped the truffles, at a temperature of 50 to 56 degrees. This will give the
ganache long enough to crystallize, and, therefore, it will not shrink away from the
tempered chocolate shell and create air pockets that can encourage the growth of mold.
Temper your chocolate as on pages 41 to 42, then transfer it to a heatproof bowl and
drop your truffles in one by one, removing them with a dipping fork or your fingers. Place
them in a bowl of cocoa powder (or whatever you've chosen to finish the truffles) or on a
plate covered with a sheet of plastic wrap.

surprise christmas trees

This idea came from a customer at Rococo who wanted to send her nieces in America some cash for Christmas. I hope they ate the trees themselves, and did not give them away! Each tree contained rolled-up $50 bills. You will need a two-piece polycarbonate mold with clips, available from good kitchenware stores. There will be lots of extra chocolate, but don't worry, as you can use it to make other things later.

3½ ounces white chocolate, melted, for the decorations (optional)

2¼ pounds tempered chocolate (pages 41 to 42; you can temper it after you have decorated the mold with white chocolate)

Prepare the mold by polishing the surface with cotton balls: the cleaner and shinier the better. The decorations are applied to the inside before it is filled rather than the molded object. Using the white chocolate, let your creative spirit loose. Either make a waxed-paper cone to pipe the decorations, or use a freehand approach with a small paintbrush. Remember that everything will come out as a mirror image, so if you are writing you should practice mirror writing. You may prepare a template and place it under the mold as a guide or work freestyle. Also, when making pairs, any decoration touching the sides needs to be matched on the pairing mold. It is probably easiest to keep away from the edges, and then you won't have to worry about this. Don't be inhibited. Try different brush marks and vary the thickness of the chocolate; with practice you can get very fine detail. Let the decorated molds dry at room temperature.

Temper the chocolate as on pages 41 to 42 and put it in a heatproof bowl set over lukewarm water. Clip the two sides of the tree mold together. Ladle the chocolate into the mold, filling it to the brim. Pour the bulk of the chocolate back into the bowl, tapping the mold. Scrape any excess from the rim, and invert the mold, so the chocolate pools in the tip; leave about 5 minutes, then check to see if the chocolate is drying. It might still look wet in places, which is fine. Repeat the process to add a second layer, which should achieve the desired thickness. Place a small surprise wrapped in cellophane (money, jewelery, or even a message or poem) into the mold, gently wedging it so it doesn't fall out when you invert the mold. You now need to make a bottom for the tree. On a side-plate size piece of paper, make a puddle of tempered chocolate a bit bigger than the bottom of tree. Press the open end of the mold into the puddle, releasing any trapped air bubbles, until it stands upright on the paper. Leave to harden 15 minutes at room temperature, then put it in the refrigerator 30 minutes. The time can vary depending on the thickness of the chocolate, and the temperature of your refrigerator. Check at intervals until you see a halo where the tempered chocolate is contracting away from the mold. At this moment take the mold out of the refrigerator; if you leave it too long, you might have problems with condensation. Peel off the paper and snap off the excess chocolate puddle, which should come away cleanly. If you can bear to leave the tree in the mold for a few hours you should achieve a glossier result. When you do unmold the tree, release the clips and tap the mold gently—in theory, the tree should just pop out.

variation

Love Hearts can be made in the same way, using the appropriate molds.

real
chocolate
delight

savory
chocolate

eggplant and tahini crostini

Well-cooked eggplants melt sweetly in the mouth in much the same way as really good chocolate; they are incredibly sensual vegetables. Many of us are put off them when they are badly prepared and either not cooked or bitter. Middle Eastern cooks understand how to treat them, perhaps better than anyone else does. This is one of my all-time favorite childhood treats, although at that time the chocolate was just a twinkle in my eye. This is the sort of recipe where the quantities do not need to be too precise; rather, trust your taste buds and adjust the flavors as you see fit.

makes 24 bite-size pieces

1 large or 2 small eggplants

4 tablespoons tahini (sesame paste)

juice of 1 or 2 lemons

2 garlic cloves, chopped

4 teaspoons unsweetened cocoa powder

large pinch of sea salt

French baguette or Italian ciabatta, for the crostini

handful of roughly chopped flat-leaf parsley, to garnish (optional)

sprinkling of smoked paprika (optional)

extra-virgin olive oil for dressing (optional)

Ideally the eggplants should be cooked whole, slowly over charcoal, but failing that they can be scorched over a naked gas flame or roasted in the oven at its hottest setting for 20 minutes, until black and collapsed; leave to cool.

Peel the skin, reserving any of the flavorful juices. Pulse the flesh and juices with the tahini, lemon juice, garlic, cocoa, and salt in a food processor or blender until you have a smooth paste. You might need to add more lemon juice or a bit of water if it seems too thick; this depends on the tahini, which can vary from being almost liquid to a fairly solid, peanut-butter consistency.

Heat the oven to 350°F. Slice the bread thinly at an angle to produce good crostini shapes. Place the slices on a baking tray and bake until crisp and golden; let cool on a wire rack. Just before serving, spread the eggplant mixture on the toasts and garnish with a little parsley and paprika, if you like. You can also dress them with a few drops of good olive oil.

beet and tahini crostini

This is very much the same as the Eggplant and Tahini Crostini on the previous page, substituting freshly cooked (not in vinegar) beets for the eggplants. The beets produce the most dramatic shade of deep pink, almost purple, when blended with the tahini. The sweet yet earthy flavor of this much-maligned root vegetable is set off by the other ingredients, and the color is set alight by a dribble of green extra-virgin olive oil and flat-leaf parsley.

crostini with goat cheese and chocolate tapenade

This recipe has been made many times and shared with friends and colleagues around the world. It is based on Claudia Roden's olive toasts—classic Mediterranean antipasti. I don't normally tell anyone about the chocolate until they have tasted these crostini, as it is difficult to discern the flavor, but it definitely adds something.

Makes about 30 pieces

1 ounce real dark chocolate, melted

1 cup pitted ripe black olives (buy 10 ounces if you are pitting them yourself)

5 preserved anchovy fillets in oil, drained and chopped

1 large garlic clove, chopped

2 tablespoons pickled capers, drained and excess vinegar squeezed out

5 tablespoons good-quality extra-virgin olive oil

2 tablespoons rum (optional)

some chopped fresh chili (optional)

French baguette or Italian ciabatta, for toast

8 ounces fresh soft goat cheese

cayenne pepper, for sprinkling

a few sprigs of dill or parsley (optional)

Put all the ingredients except the bread, goat cheese, cayenne, and herbs in a food processor or blender, and pulse until everything is mixed but still retains some texture. Make the toasts as described on the previous page and leave to cool on a wire rack. Just before serving, spread the tapenade on the toasts; then place a thin slice of goat cheese on top, and finish with a sprinkle of cayenne and a herb leaf.

chocolate sushi

This recipe was presented at a chocolate master class given at the Eurochoc Festival in Perugia, Italy. I assisted *chef chocolatier* Paul de Bondt and chef Alessandro Battistero, and the sushi uses my chocolate tapenade in its middle. Making sushi looks very daunting first time around, but it's actually simple. The sushi vinegar, nori, umeboshi, wasabi, pickled vinegar, and sushi mat can all be bought in specialist Japanese stores, some health-food stores, many larger supermarkets, and department store cookware departments. If you can't find toasted nori, toast it yourself, lightly, over a gas burner. The accompanying Salt and Pepper Chocolate can be made well in advance if you prefer.

makes 24 pieces

1½ cups Japanese rice

6 tablespoons sushi vinegar, plus more for your hands

4 large sheets of toasted nori seaweed

12 drained canned anchovy fillets

½ cucumber, peeled, halved, seeded, and cut into long strips

8 umeboshi plums, quartered, pitted, and cut into strips, or 4 tablespoons umeboshi paste (optional)

for the chocolate tapenade

5 ounces pitted black olives (for the best flavor, buy big, juicy kalamata olives and pit them yourself; if you can't be bothered, use canned pitted olives)

1 garlic clove, roughly chopped

2 tablespoons pickled capers, drained and roughly chopped

1 ounce real dark chocolate, melted

for the salt and pepper chocolate

5 ounces tempered chocolate (pages 40-41)

1 teaspoon flaked sea salt

1 teaspoon cracked black pepper

to serve

wasabi (Japanese horseradish)

pickled ginger

for the dipping sauce

4 tablespoons light soy sauce

1 tablespoon dry sherry or mirin

First prepare the rice: Soak it in cold water for 10 minutes; drain any excess water. Put the rice into a heavy-bottomed pan and add 1½ cups fresh cold water. Bring to a boil; turn down the heat and simmer, covered, 6 to 7 minutes, until just tender and all the water is absorbed. Fluff up the rice with a fork and place in a large, flat dish or baking tray. Add the sushi vinegar and mix well with a spatula, fanning the rice to cool it quickly. (In Japanese sushi kitchens, there is someone whose job it is just to fan the rice!) When cool, put to one side.

Prepare the tapenade by processing all the ingredients together in a food processor or blender to make a rough paste.

To assemble the sushi, place a sheet of toasted nori shiny side down on a bamboo sushi mat. With vinegared hands, spread one-quarter of the rice evenly over the entire width and two-thirds of the depth of the nori. Arrange a row of anchovies and tapenade along the middle of the rice across the width, and put the cucumber strips on top, together with the umeboshi plums or paste, if using.

Using the mat, roll up the nori to make a cylinder about $1\frac{1}{2}$ inches in diameter, then press it in the rolled mat to form it into a square shape. Repeat with the other pieces of nori and remaining ingredients. Using a sharp knife, cut each piece in half, then cut each of these into 3 equal pieces.

To make the Salt and Pepper Chocolate, spread the tempered chocolate as thinly as possible on a sheet of Cellophane or on a tray covered in plastic wrap (but make sure it won't slip around). Sprinkle the salt and pepper as evenly as possible over the surface of the chocolate. When it has started to cool, divide it into squares about $1\frac{3}{4}$ inches and leave on the sheet to finish cooling in the refrigerator.

Carefully arrange the sushi pieces on a serving dish and spear each with a piece of Salt and Pepper Chocolate. Serve with a small mountain of wasabi, some pickled ginger, and the dipping sauce made by mixing the soy sauce and sherry or mirin.

chocolate tempura

Well-made and really freshly served tempura is a rare treat. It is possible to make it in a domestic kitchen, but always use fresh oil, and cook the tempura in very small batches to keep the oil at the right temperature. An electric deep fryer is a great help, but you can also use a wok or a deep, heavy-bottomed pan. Serve each batch immediately and carry on cooking! You can batter and deep-fry almost anything, from Mars Bars to quail eggs. Choose whatever you want, but don't cook just one thing; a selection of four or five ingredients is best. The basic batter recipe comes from Madhur Jaffrey's *Eastern Vegetarian Cooking*. Cocoa nibs are the raw material from which chocolate is made; they come from the whole beans that have been nibbed or cracked. Very nutty, they give great texture to savory dishes.

serves 4

20 string beans

12 shelled and deveined raw jumbo
   shrimps

8 baby artichokes, quartered

8 baby eggplants

8 asparagus spears

thin end of a butternut squash, peeled
   and thinly sliced

8 whole scallions

2 red bell peppers

1 medium-size squid, cleaned and cut
   into rings

2 sweet potatoes

8 ounces raw tuna tenderloin, cut into
   chunks

7 ounces firm tofu, cut into strips

grapeseed, peanut, or sunflower oil
   for deep-frying

for the dipping sauce

1 tablespoon soy sauce

4 tablespoons sake

2 tablespoons Chocolate-Balsamic
   Vinegar (page 60)

$\frac{2}{3}$ cup dashi or good-quality vegetable
   stock, or dried-mushroom soaking water

2 tablespoons grated fresh ginger root

8 ounces daikon (mooli), grated

for the batter

1 large egg yolk

2 cups ice-cold water

1$\frac{2}{3}$ cups all-purpose flour

2 ounces cocoa nibs (see above)

handful of chopped fresh cilantro

1 or 2 small, fresh chilies, seeded and
   chopped, or more to taste

to serve

tube of wasabi

First make the dipping sauce: Mix together the soy sauce, mirin, vinegar, and dashi.

Prepare the batter by beating the egg yolk in a bowl until smooth, then beat in the ice-cold water. Finally add the flour, cocoa nibs, cilantro, and chilies. Beat briefly, but the mixture should still be lumpy. (If you overmix, it will be tough when cooked!) Leave to stand 10 minutes while you heat the oil in a wok or deep fryer.

Meanwhile, prepare any vegetables that are too large to cook whole, slicing them into very even slices so they all cook at the same rate. Flour any wet ingredients before dipping them into the batter. Heat the oil until just beginning to smoke (375°F). Fry small batches of one sort of vegetable or fish at a time. Drain on paper towels before serving.

Stir the ginger and daikon into the dipping sauce. Serve the sauce and wasabi with the tempura.

chocolate-balsamic vinegar

I have found this little invention totally invaluable. As well as its obvious uses, say in salad dressings or to deglaze pans to make gravies and sauces, you will see it delivers the chocolate element in lots of my savory recipes. It does, however, also lend itself to dishes other than savory–just try it over fresh strawberries. For a more piquant version to use with red-meat and cheese dishes, like Welsh rabbit, add 7 tablespoons Worcestershire sauce.

Makes about 1 cup

½ cup superfine sugar

7 tablespoons vinegar (I use equal parts apple cider and cooking balsamic)

1 ounce real dark chocolate, grated

Gently heat the sugar and vinegar in a small, deep pan until all the sugar dissolves, then leave to bubble slowly, 5 minutes.

Take the pan off the heat, and whisk in the chocolate well; leave to cool. When cool, stir again quickly. Pour into a small, clean jelly jar, seal, and store until needed.

james's 5-minute chocolate deviled kidneys

This is one of my husband's favorite dishes, and was in the Booth family repertoire before he was born. I let him make it because I hate cutting up kidneys. In fact, I would have sworn that I hated kidneys until James made me taste these (the same recipe sans chocolate). When he was a small boy, his father would be served this dish for supper as a special treat while all the boys waited on the sidelines for a "bonus." James's mother cooks the kidneys for about half an hour, but I think that, like squid, they can be flash-fried in a wok in a couple of minutes and be just as good—if not better.

serves 2

6 to 8 lamb kidneys (preferably organic)

2 teaspoons Dijon mustard

1 tablespoon tomato paste

2 teaspoons oyster sauce

1 glass of dry sherry, sake, or red wine

1 teaspoon anchovy essence

2 tablespoons grapeseed oil or olive oil

1 onion, chopped

1 or 2 garlic cloves, thinly sliced

2 teaspoons unsweetened cocoa powder

black pepper or cayenne pepper, to taste

to serve

steamed basmati or Thai rice, or toast

crème fraîche (optional)

a handful of flat-leaf parsley

Prepare the kidneys by halving them and removing the white cores very carefully. Stir the mustard, tomato paste, oyster sauce, sherry, and anchovy essence together to make sauce; set aside.

Heat the oil in a hot wok over medium-high heat, and quickly fry the onion and garlic; set aside. Flash-fry the kidneys 2 minutes, then return the onions to the pan, together with the sauce, cocoa, and pepper or cayenne to taste. Cook until the sauce is bubbling and has the consistency of light cream: If it is too thick, add more wine.

Serve with steamed basmati or Thai rice. Add a dollop of crème fraîche, if you like, and some flat-leaf parsley. Alternatively, the kidneys are also delicious on toast as a traditional British after-dinner savory–or for breakfast. If you can't stand kidneys, use mushrooms.

green henry

This is a traditional northern German recipe, made by my old friend Ariane Severin. I enjoyed it very much and thought it a suitable case for a chocolate spin. Though it's normally made in the summer, with freshly picked beans and underripe pears, I serve this as a dish on its own or as a vegetable accompaniment to meat, fowl, game, or sausages.

serves 4 to 6

1 pound slab Canadian bacon or Italian pancetta in a piece, cut into rough cubes

1 tablespoon olive oil

1 tablespoon butter

2¼ pounds freshly picked green beans (string or thin green beans)

1 pound small, unripe pears, with their skins left on

1 glass of red wine

2 tablespoons balsamic vinegar

salt and pepper

1 ounce real dark chocolate, finely chopped

freshly grated nutmeg

handful of chopped parsley

In a large saucepan, fry the bacon or pancetta in a little oil and butter until well cooked, and then remove any excess fat from the pan. Remove the tops from beans, but there's no need to take off the tails. Put the beans and the whole pears on top of the bacon; cover with 2¼ cups water, the wine, and the vinegar, but do not stir. Cover the pan and leave to simmer about 40 minutes, or until the pears are cooked through.

To serve, arrange a pile of beans and bacon on each plate and top with a whole pear. Boil the sauce in the pan to reduce by about half, then season with pepper and stir in the chocolate. Pour some of the sauce over each pear and sprinkle the beans with a grating of nutmeg and parsley.

hangover fried eggs

This quick dish is perfect at any time of the day or night—and is especially good for chasing away hangovers! Put a knob of butter in a skillet. When it's sizzling and starting to turn black at the edge, slide one or two eggs into the pan, sprinkle with salt and pepper, and cook to taste—I like mine over easy (turned over and cooked briefly on the other side). Put the eggs on a warm plate and deglaze the pan with a tablespoon of Chocolate-Balsamic Vinegar (page 60). Crusty bread and salad turn this into a more substantial dish.

james's real guacamole

My husband, James, traveled in Mexico as a student and now declares no one in England knows how to make "real" guacamole. In this, garlic, cream cheese, sour cream, and other spurious ingredients are banned. It is actually very easy and delicious. Possibly a little chopped fresh cilantro is permissible. There's no chocolate in this recipe! It is, however, the perfect foil to the black beans on page 81, and a great addition to any of the other chocolate mezze.

serves 4

2 ripe avocados

juice of 1 lemon or 2 limes

2 ripe tomatoes, blanched in boiling water

and skinned

½ red onion, minced

really good pinch of sea salt

½ small red fresh chili, seeded and minced, or cayenne pepper, to taste

Scoop the flesh out of the avocados, keeping the pits, and put into a bowl. Cover with lemon or lime juice and mash lightly with a fork—it doesn't need to be a smooth puree.

Skin the tomatoes, slice in half horizontally, and squeeze out and discard the seeds and juice. Remove any hard or pithy bits of flesh and chop finely. Mix this, the onion, salt, and chili into the avocado. If you don't want to eat this immediately, put the pits back into the guacamole and chill in the refrigerator. This stops the guacamole from turning brown.

eggplant, chocolate, and goat cheese pizzettes

The eggplant mixture is based on the Sicilian caponata and uses sweet-n-sour elements of vinegar and chocolate to complement the eggplant. The pizzette crust and goat cheese are among my all-time-favorite ingredients.

These baby pizzas can be assembled and cooked at the last minute, if you have prepared all the ingredients beforehand, making them perfect finger food. Make the dough in the morning or the night before if you are having this for lunch.

If you haven't got the time to make the chocolate-flavored vinegar, or don't want to be bothered, you can sprinkle the cooked eggplants with some unsweetened cocoa powder and balsamic vinegar before assembling the pizzettes.

Makes about 8 to 10 small pizzettes

for the pizza dough

- 2²/₃ cups 00 (Italian doppio zero) flour
- 1½ teaspoons sugar
- 1 tablespoon fast-rise instant yeast
  (about 1³/₄ envelopes)
- 1 cup ice-cold water
- 1½ teaspoons salt

for the topping

- 2 eggplants, each about 12 ounces
- 1 big red onion, finely chopped
- 2 garlic cloves, finely chopped
- ½ fennel bulb, finely chopped
- 1 tablespoon olive oil, plus more for the
  eggplant
- 1 tablespoon butter
- 6 tomatoes, skinned, or 1 large can of
  peeled plum tomatoes
- semolina or all-purpose flour for dusting
- 7 ounces fresh goat cheese
- handful of good black olives, pitted
  and halved
- 2 tablespoons miniature capers
- 7 ounces cheddar cheese, grated
  mozzarella or other cheese, chopped
- ²/₃ cup pine nuts
- handful of chopped flat-leaf parsley
- about 1 tablespoon Chocolate-Balsamic
  Vinegar (page 60)
- sprinkling of smoked paprika (optional)

Make the dough, in a large bowl, mix the flour with the sugar and yeast, trying not to let them come into direct contact. Add some ice-cold water, knead, and then add the salt.

Knead quickly, adding water as necessary, until you have a ball of elastic dough; takes about 5 minutes. Cover the dough with plastic wrap and put it into the refrigerator immediately. Leave it an hour or two. (This way of making the dough lets the yeast and flavors develop very slowly, and when you roll it out, it will burst into life.)

Prepare the topping: Cut the eggplants into quarters lengthways and then into ½ inch slices. Salt the slices and leave to "sweat" in a colander.

Meanwhile, sauté the onion, garlic, and fennel in the olive oil and butter over low heat 10 to 15 minutes. Add the tomatoes with their liquid and simmer another 10 to 15 minutes until the sauce has a thick, saucelike consistency.

The eggplants will now be discolored and covered in droplets of moisture. Pat the eggplants dry with paper towel and then shallow-fry in as little olive oil as possible in a large skillet, until brown on both sides and well-cooked, about 5 minutes. You might need to do this in batches.

Heat the oven to the hottest setting. Oil several cookie sheets, then dust them with semolina. Whiz the tomato sauce with a hand-held mixer and get the dough out of the refrigerator. Cut the dough into 8–10 pieces, roll each out as thinly as possible into 6-inch circles, and arrange on the cookie sheets. (You can even make miniature ones in tartlet pans.) Cover the pizzettes with tomato sauce and arrange the eggplant, crumbled goat cheese, olives, and capers on top. Sprinkle with grated cheese and pine nuts and bake 10 to 15 minutes, until crisp.

Just before serving, drizzle the chocolate-flavored vinegar over the pizzettes, followed by some flat-leaf parsley and smoked paprika, if you like.

reverend mother's arm

At boarding school we used to be served a steamed roly-poly suet pudding with jam in the middle, which we took to calling "Reverend Mother's arm"! I have used this idea to make a savory pasta roll—to which you can give your own name.

In the past I have made this for 30 people, but you need a large kitchen and big fish kettles to work on that scale. The advantage of making this roll rather than stuffing ravioli is that there is no danger of losing the filling when the ravioli explode in the cooking liquid, which does seem to happen, even for the most experienced of old pasta hands. You can also bake this roll in the oven, covered with a béchamel sauce.

Feel free to experiment with different fillings—roast pumpkin also works very well. You can have up to four sorts of filling, depending on how elaborate you want it to be!

for 8

for the pasta

2 fresh large eggs (newly laid if possible)

1⅓ cups 00 (Italian doppio zero) flour

1 tablespoon unsweetened cocoa powder

a very little ice-cold water

about 1 ounce cocoa nibs

for the mushroom filling

2 ounces dried porcini (ceps), soaked in boiling water to cover and left 1 hour

1 small red onion, chopped

1 tablespoon butter

1 tablespoon olive oil

3 cups roughly chopped cremini mushrooms

salt and pepper

for the spinach and ricotta filling

1 pound spinach

½ cup ricotta cheese

¾ cup crumbly blue cheese, such as Stilton, crumbled

freshly grated nutmeg

for the beet and goat cheese filling

about 1 pound raw or cooked (as long as not vinegared) beets

½ cup ricotta cheese

4 ounces goat cheese

to serve

⅔ cup pine nuts, toasted, to garnish

1 cup (2 sticks) unsalted butter

big handful of fresh sage leaves

Make the pasta: Sift the flour and cocoa powder into a food processor, then add the eggs and blend to a smooth ball of dough. (If too dry, add a little ice-cold water.) You can also make and knead this dough by hand. Wrap in plastic wrap and chill while you make the fillings.

To make the mushroom filling, drain the porcini, reserving the liquid. Squeeze the excess liquid out of the mushrooms and chop. Sauté the onion in the butter and olive oil over very low heat about 15 minutes—don't let it brown. Add the porcini and fresh mushrooms, and cook another 5 minutes. If they start to get too dry at any point, add some of the strained porcini soaking water. Season and leave to cool.

To make the spinach and ricotta filling, cook the spinach 2 to 3 minutes, either by steaming it or blanching it in boiling water. Drain, squeeze out as much water as possible, and chop roughly. Mix it with the cheeses. Season to taste with salt, pepper, and nutmeg.

To make the beet and goat cheese filling, you can use cooked beets as long as they were not cooked in vinegar–or cook your own. Do not pierce the beets, but test to see if they are cooked by trying to peel back the skin with your thumb—if you can do this, the beet is cooked. Leave to cool, then peel. Chop roughly, and mix with the cheeses and seasoning.

To assemble the "arm," if using a pasta machine, cut the dough into several equal-size pieces. If you do not have a machine, roll the entire ball of dough by hand into a very smooth, large rectangle as thin as possible (about $\frac{1}{16}$th of an inch). If making by machine, the strips need to be "welded" together using a little water, again until you have a sheet about 18x12 inches. The seams should be at right angles to the rolling edge, or the "arm" might fall apart.

Carefully place the dough on a clean dish towel. Scatter the cocoa nibs over the dough and then spread the different mixtures evenly in stripes across it, leaving a blank strip about 2 inches wide at the end and sides to seal. Start by rolling the filled end, using the towel to help if necessary. When rolled up, seal side and ends by dampening the edges with cold water and pressing firmly. Roll up in the towel and tie with string, so it looks like a beef tenderloin.

To cook, immerse in boiling salted water and simmer 30 minutes. Meanwhile, toast the pine nuts gently until golden. Make a sage butter by melting the butter in a pan, dropping in the sage, and cooking for a few minutes. To serve, untie the bundle and cut into slices (ideally 2 per person), discarding the ends. Serve with the sage butter and toasted pine nuts.

quick pan-roasted chicken with chocolate vinegar

One of my "black beasts" is fast food, meaning the kind of stuff peddled to children on every shopping street in the developed world. It makes me angry on many counts: the cynical exploitation of children as a target audience, the apparent inability of parents to resist "pester power," the nutritional paucity of the offering, and then the exploitation of cheap labor and cheaply raised-factory-farmed animals*. This is my attempt to win my small children over with my version–and pander to their love of vinegar!

First, find a happily raised chicken, preferably organic or free-range, jointed. In a non-stick pan, cook the chicken on very high heat for 5 minutes on each side until brown. Pour off any fat, season with salt, pepper, and some fines herbes, and garlic if your children like it. Cover and continue to cook until the pieces are thoroughly cooked, about 10 minutes longer. Remove the chicken pieces and leave them to rest for a few minutes. Collect any juices that have run from them (these should be clear—if pink, the chicken is not cooked through). Deglaze the pan with Chocolate-Balsamic Vinegar (page 60) and the juices. Pour this sauce over the chicken. Serve with rice and a salad.

*I heartily recommend anyone interested in these issues to read *Fast Food Nation* by Eric Schlosser (Houghton Mifflin, 2001, ISBN 0-713-99602-1), which is a compelling read and very scary.

paul de Bondt's mignon di pasta ripieni con passate di lentichhie (lentil puree with raviolini)

serves 8 to 10 as a first course

for the lentil puree

1 cup brown lentils (ideally Castellucci)

1 onion, minced

2 garlic cloves, minced

1 carrot, minced

½ celery stalk, minced

1 tablespoon olive oil

1 tablespoon ras el hanout spices (optional)

small handful of fresh sage

small sprig of rosemary

2 bay leaves

for the pasta

3 extra-large, very fresh eggs, plus 1 extra yolk

salt

3⅓ cups 00 (Italian doppio zero) flour

½ tablespoon olive oil, plus more for drizzling

Chocolate-Balsamic Vinegar (page 60), for drizzling

coarse semolina for dusting

for the stuffing

5 ounces bread

9 ounces lean pork fillet

9 ounces sausage meat

2 tablespoons ground toasted hazelnuts

1½ ounces cocoa nibs (page 59)

salt and pepper

First make the lentil puree (this tastes best when made earlier): Soften the vegetables in olive oil over very low heat until golden, about 10 minutes, but do not let them brown. Add the ras el hanout and fry for 1 minute. Cover with water (about twice the volume of the lentils) and bring to a simmer, then cook 20 minutes to 1 hour, checking regularly until the lentils are al dente. Strain any excess water and reserve. Remove the herbs; divide the lentils in 2 portions and puree one half. Add to the whole lentils and bring to a boil; set aside and leave to cool. Adjust seasoning to taste, and adjust its thickness with the reserved lentil water—it should be denser than soup.

Make the pasta dough: Put the eggs, salt, flour, and oil into the food processor and blend into a ball of dough. It should be rather stiff, although you can add a little water if you need to. Wrap in plastic wrap and set aside, to allow to rest while you make the stuffing.

Prepare the stuffing: Soak the bread in water and squeeze dry. Process this with all the other stuffing ingredients, except the cocoa nibs, in a food processor until roughly chopped. Break up the cocoa nibs with a rolling pin and mix into the meat; season to taste.

Either by hand or with a pasta machine, roll the pasta into very thin sheets. (Lydia Sodani, a superwoman married to a farmer with a Parmesan herd in Reggio Emilia, showed me how to make ravioli. The texture needs to be silky smooth, and you can only achieve this by repeated rolling. On the machine, I put it through 6 or 7 times on the widest setting until very smooth. Between each passing, fold the sheet into as neat a rectangle as you can to insure a regular shape that's then easy to work on the second smallest setting to get the final sheet. You might need extra flour to stop the dough from sticking.) When you have made your sheets, cut into 4–5 inch squares. Place a spoonful of stuffing into the middle of each, and seal the edges using a damp pastry brush (don't overwet!). Fold corner to corner and press down firmly to create a triangle. Trim the edges if necessary. Sprinkle a tray with coarse semolina and place the ravioli on it. They can be made a few hours ahead. There should be 3 per person.

Cook the ravioli in lots of gently boiling salted water until the pasta is al dente, about 20 minutes—test by cutting off a bit of border. (Some people say 4 minutes, but Lydia always cooks hers for much longer, usually 20, and so do I—it depends how thick the pasta is. Start testing from about 10 minutes.) Take out of the pan individually and drain in a colander. Place in a warm skillet with some olive oil and gently toss until gleaming. Serve 3 per portion on top of a mound of reheated lentil puree. Finish with a drizzle of oil and vinegar.

lacquered duck in chocolate sauce

This is Paul de Bondt's recipe, which he demonstrated in his chocolate master class during the Eurochocolate Festival in Perugia, Italy, in 2000. I was guest chef part of the time, when I was not being commandeered to do tutored chocolate tastings with the delegates of the "chocohouse" school. Paul began as a chef in Holland, and then fell in love with Italy, the Italians, and one Italian in particular, Cecilia Iacobelli. They now own and run one of the very finest artisan chocolate stores in Italy.

Paul is full of energy and good ideas; he loves to brainstorm, and shares his knowledge and enthusiasm about food, wine, and chocolate with fellow professionals in a spirit I find so refreshing. I have spent many inspiring hours in his company. Paul and Cecilia often prepare chocolate banquets, and this is one of the dishes they might serve, although it needs plenty of time and planning in the preparation. My chocolate tapenade is often featured, too. (See the Chocolate Sushi on page 55.) Good accompaniments for the duck include marinated ginger (bought) mixed with pieces of orange, orange juice, and cooked orange peel cut in julienne strips, then served ice-cold in small bowls; fried soy noodles; onions and zucchini, stir-fried in a wok; or curly raw leeks. All should be finished with toasted black and white sesame seeds.

Serves 8

1 fine fresh duck, weighing about 3⅓ pounds

¼ cup sugar

50g honey

big lump of gingerroot, peeled and sliced into little strips

12 whole cardamom pods

a little licorice root or powder (optional)

for the sauce

reserved giblets, neck, and wing tips of the duck

2 tablespoons oil

1 onion, roughly chopped

1 celery stalk, roughly chopped

1 carrot, roughly chopped

1 tablespoon soy sauce

small glass of dry sherry

1 ounce bittersweet chocolate or real dark chocolate

cornstarch (optional)

To prepare the duck, make a small hole in skin and blow up the poor beast with a compressor or a drinking straw. This lifts the skin, so the fat underneath drains out during cooking and the skin becomes beautifully crisp. Cut off the neck and wing tips and reserve.

Make a thick syrup by boiling the sugar, honey, and 1¼ cups water together. Then add the ginger and cardamom, together with a little licorice if you can find it! Paint the syrup on the duck and hang it in a cool, airy place (not the refrigerator) until the end of the day. Keep painting it with the syrup whenever you think about it.

Heat the oven to 350°F. Place the duck on a rack over a roasting pan filled with water. Cook the duck until it is well roasted and caramelized, 1½ to 2 hours.

To make the sauce, brown the duck neck and wing tips in a little oil in a heavy-bottomed saucepan. Add the onion, celery, and carrots, and fry gently for a few minutes. Make a stock by adding the giblets, together with the ginger and cardamom taken from the sugar syrup and 1¼ cups water. Boil for several hours, until the sauce has reduced by half; strain and skim any fat from the top. Now add the soy sauce, dry sherry, and finally the chocolate to taste. This is the most critical part of the recipe—add the chocolate little by little, and stop when you can discern the bitterness. If it needs to be thickened, add a little cornstarch mixed with cold water and boil until the sauce is no longer cloudy.

hare and chocolate sauce

Hare and chocolate are inextricably linked for me, as some of the most beautiful Easter molds depict hares. Long before the Christian feast of Easter existed, the roman dawn goddess Oestre was a symbol of new life and spring. She was said to disguise herself as a hare and go around hiding eggs behind bushes–hence Easter egg hunts.

Quite apart from that, the meat of the hare goes exceptionally well with chocolate. It is very dark, extremely lean, and needs long cooking. I have tried several ways of cooking hare, and the best, in my opinion, is to make a ragu with it, to be served with tagliatelle. My son, aged 5, pronounced it delicious and said he'd like to eat it for supper every night! This recipe is an Italian classic, and different versions can be found in many books, this one is probably closest to that served at the River Café in London. This recipe offers a change from spring lamb at Easter time. The chocolate gives body to the sauce. In Italy, particularly in Sicily, chocolate is often added to *agrodolce* dishes—combining sweet and sour flavors. If you can't get hare, use a couple of rabbits.

serves 4 as a stew, plus 4 to 6 as a pasta sauce

1 hare, weighing around 5 pounds, jointed
(ask butcher to remove any small bones
and ribs and try to get the blood and liver)
flour
salt and pepper
4 tablespoons olive oil
handful of pickled walnuts or capers
  (optional)
3½ ounces Italian pancetta, cubed
12 shallots, finely chopped
4 garlic cloves, finely chopped
1 small fennel bulb, cored and chopped
3 large carrots, chopped

2 ounces real dark chocolate or 4½
  tablespoons unsweetened cocoa powder
2 fourteen-and-a-half-ounce cans
  crushed tomatoes (if making pasta sauce)
big handful of roughly chopped parsley

for the marinade

1 bottle of good red wine
6 bay leaves
5 whole star anise
½ teaspoon fennel seeds (optional)

to serve as a pasta sauce

1 pound tagliatelle, cooked
pesto sauce, to dress
freshly grated Parmesan cheese

You can eat this as a casserole first, then use the leftovers for a pasta sauce. Either way, start by marinating the hare overnight (time permitting) in the wine, with the bay leaves, star anise, and fennel seeds, if using.

Dry the hare, then dust it with the seasoned flour. Brown each piece in a little of the oil in a heavy-bottomed pan. Then add the marinade (with a little water, if necessary, to cover) and the pickled walnuts and bring to a boil. Reduce the heat and simmer for as long as the hare needs to become really tender—this can actually be anything from 1 to 8 hours, depending on the age and condition of the hare.

While the hare is cooking, dry-fry the pancetta until golden. Add the shallots, garlic, fennel, carrots, and olive oil and sauté slowly, until the carrots are tender. Add all of these to the hare, together with the chocolate or cocoa, and simmer 15 minutes longer. (If serving as "jugged hare," the blood and liver should be pureed in a blender or food processor and added with the chocolate.) Adjust the seasoning to taste. Mashed potatoes and roasted root vegetables, such as beets and parsnips, suit this dish.

If you are planning to serve the hare as a ragu, after cooking it in the marinade until tender, take the pieces of hare out the sauce and remove any bones, the star anise, and the bay leaves. Cook until reduced somewhat. Meanwhile, in a food processor, chop the leg meat finely, then shred the saddle (not in the processor), leaving some reasonably big pieces. Return the chopped meat to the sauce and add the cooked onion mixture, the tomatoes, parsley, and chocolate. Cook until the sauce has reduced and is thick and rich-looking. Adjust the seasoning to taste. Serve with tagliatelle dressed with some pesto and freshly grated Parmesan.

mexican refried beans with chocolate sauce

This is a variation on the Venezuelan staple *caraotas*. Eaten "out there" (as the colonials would say), it is usually served as a breakfast dish, with *arepas*, a white-corn griddle cake, white cheese, and fried eggs. At home, we often have this as a brunch dish. It takes a few days to make and tastes best after three or four days. If you don't have much time, pressure cook the beans without even presoaking them. This way you can cook them one day and eat them the next.

Serve these with many other dishes, such as chicken (see the pan-seared chicken recipe on page 71); soft tortillas; or scrambled, poached, or fried eggs with chocolate-flavored vinegar; bacon; or crumbly white cheese, such as British Wensleydale, the cheese recently been given such a boost by Wallace & Grommit.

1¼ cups small black beans from South
  America (not black-eyed peas)

2 red onions, roughly chopped

3 garlic cloves, roughly chopped

1 tablespoon olive oil

1 tablespoon butter

a good 2-inch chunk of very fresh
  ginger, finely chopped or grated

1 fresh red chili, seeded and
  finely chopped, or more to taste

1 cup tomato puree

4½ tablespoons unsweetened cocoa
  powder or chocolate

fresh cilantro leaves or flat-leaf
  parsley, to garnish

Two days ahead, put the beans to soak overnight in cold water to cover.

Next day, drain, cover with fresh water, bring to a simmer, and simmer until really tender.

Gently sauté the onions and garlic in olive oil and butter 10 minutes or so, until golden. Add the ginger and chili, and cook 1 to 2 minutes longer. Add the drained cooked beans and the tomato puree. Season with salt and pepper and leave overnight for the flavors to develop.

Next day, simmer gently for an hour. Stir in the cocoa or chocolate and garnish with the cilantro just before serving.

Roast lamb with chocolate, anchovies, and capers

This is a very rich dish. I recommend serving it with steamed basmati rice or new potatoes and a green salad.

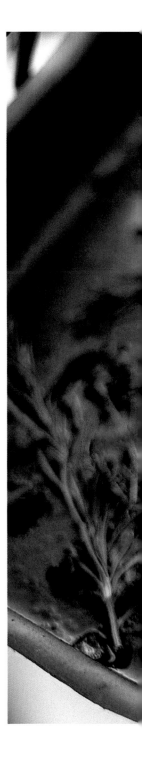

Serves 8 to 10

1 whole leg of lamb, about 4 pounds

1 large onion, roughly chopped

small bunch of fresh rosemary

sprig or 2 of fresh thyme

1 ounce real dark chocolate, or 5½ tablespoons unsweetened cocoa powder

for the marinade

1 glass of red wine or sherry

1 teaspoon good olive oil

2 tablespoons tiny capers

2 teaspoons strong Dijon mustard

4 to 6 anchovy fillets (bottled or canned)

handful of chopped parsley

2 large garlic cloves

black pepper

If you have time to marinate the lamb overnight it improves the flavor and texture of the meat, but even an hour will make a difference. In a blender, make a marinade with the wine or sherry, oil, capers, mustard, anchovies, parsley, garlic, and pepper. With a sharp knife, make slashes in the lamb every 2 to 2½ inches, about ½ inch deep. Massage the marinade into the lamb. Put into a roasting pan, cover with foil, and leave in a cool place.

When ready to cook, heat the oven to 375°F. Put the chopped onion in a small mound at the bottom of the pan with a sprig of rosemary. Put the lamb on top of the mound of onions. Sprinkle the rest of the rosemary and thyme on top of the meat. Put in the oven and bake 20 minutes per 1¼ pounds for pink, 30 for medium, or until cooked to your taste. Take the lamb out of the oven and leave to stand in a warm place, loosely covered with foil, 10 to 15 minutes.

Make a gravy by scraping up the onion and any other juices in the pan or from the meat. Take out the rosemary and add more wine, if you like. When you have a thick sauce, add the chocolate or cocoa and stir in well; it should thicken the sauce a little and give a deep color and aroma. Strain or simply remove any very burned pieces of onion before serving.

desserts
&
drinks

river cafe chocolate nemesis revisited

I have long admired London's River Café Italian restaurant from a distance and via the books of Rose Gray and Ruth Rogers. They have a wonderfully clear vision of how to prepare and serve food at its best, and they have certainly revolutionized many kitchens in the UK and around the world. There seems hardly to be a self-respecting chef in England who has not worked at the restaurant at some time in his or her career.

I had a surprise birthday lunch there recently and was absolutely delighted when Ruth Rogers came to the table and declared Rococo to be her favorite shop. She then took me to meet Rose Gray, and we talked chocolate for some time. Which chocolate did I use? What do they use? We all tasted some pretty raw chocolate from a plantation in Venezuela that they had been given and were experimenting with. Even in its raw state, the quality of its cocoa beans shone through this chocolate.

I had been dying to taste their celebrated Chocolate Nemesis, and so we shared it for pudding. At the end of the meal, Ruth and Rose asked me what I thought of the pudding. Here I was, in front of these two gurus of modern Italian food, being asked my opinion of one of their most famous creations. I said it was really delicious, extremely rich and filling (we were unable to finish it), the texture sublime, but that I found it perhaps a little too sweet and buttery. Finally I asked if, with their blessing, I could tweak the recipe and put it into my book. I have changed the method of assembling the ingredients, but this seems to produce the correct texture, so here it is.

makes 6 large or 12 normal portions

1 cup sifted confectioners' sugar

4 large organic eggs, separated

9 ounces real dark chocolate (I used Valrhona Guanaja 70%), roughly chopped

²/₃ cup butter (1¼ sticks), cut into small pieces, plus more for greasing

pinch of salt

1 teaspoon apple cider vinegar

crème fraîche, to serve

Heat the oven to 350°F and line the base of an 8-inch round cake pan (not springform) that is 2 inches deep with parchment paper.

Put two-thirds of the sugar in a heavy-bottomed pan with 5 tablespoons water. Heat until the sugar completely dissolves. Then, over low heat, add the chocolate and stir until it melts. Finally, stir in the butter: You should have a thick, glossy mixture. Remove from the heat and set aside.

Whisk the remaining sugar with the egg white, salt, and vinegar (I don't know why this works, but it does seem to help) until they reach meringue/soft-peak consistency. Beat the egg yolks into the lukewarm chocolate mixture and add this mixture to your meringue, folding it in gently, bit by bit.

Bring a large kettleful of water to a boil and pour into a roasting pan large enough to hold the cake pan, to make a bain-marie. Pour the batter into the pan and place it in the roasting pan: It is important that the water comes up to the rim of the cake pan. Carefully place in the oven and bake 30 minutes, or until set. Test by placing you hand gently on the surface, or with a skewer; it should be set like a firm jelly.

Leave to cool completely out of the water bath before removing from the pan. Serve cold with crème fraîche.

Bad girl's trifle

The antithesis of an old-fashioned British trifle made from sponge cake, canned peaches, jelly, thick custard, and a spot of sherry, this one is for "bad girls." You can make a quick version using bottled or canned pears, store-bought custard, and trifle sponges, or you can go the whole hog and make your own poached pears, custard sauce, and bake cake fingers—I'll leave that up to you.

serves at least 12

7 ounces real dark chocolate, finely chopped

⅔ cup boiling water

3 to 4 tablespoons Morello cherry jelly

1 package of trifle sponge fingers (8 pieces) or pound cake, cut into eight 3x1 inch slices, each about ½ inch thick

2 jars of pears in their juice (about 14 ounces pears, 1¾ cups juice)

a good slug of poire Williams (a pear-flavored *eau-de-vie)* or vodka

2¼ cups store-bought custard sauce

1 cup whipping cream

1 cup plain yogurt

to decorate

unsweetened cocoa powder

chocolate curls, leaves, or flakes (page 43)

Make a water ganache (page 32), using the chopped chocolate and the boiling water, then set aside.

Spread a thin layer of cherry jelly on the trifle sponges and arrange them at the bottom of a glass dish or large salad bowl. Strain the pears and reserve the juice. Mix the juice with a good slug of eau de vie or vodka, and pour over the sponges. Put a layer of pears on the sponge fingers. Now pour the custard sauce over the pears. Very gently pour the cooled chocolate ganache over the layer of custard. Leave to cool for an hour or so in the refrigerator.

Just before serving, whip the cream until reasonably stiff. Fold in the yogurt and spread on top of the chocolate. Decorate with chocolate curls, leaves, and flake, then dust with cocoa powder sifted through a fine sifter.

white chocolate pannacotta with saffron and cardamom

This is my idea of Italian nursery food, especially when combined with white chocolate. My theory is that white chocolate is one the closest things to breast milk (see page 23); at least most small children I know seem to think so. It could be served with all sorts of things other than the chocolate sauce, particularly a sharp fruit such as rhubarb, plum or raspberry.

serves 6

2 gelatin leaves

½ teaspoon saffron strands

2¼ cups whipping cream

1 vanilla bean, split

12 whole cardamom pods, bruised

7 ounces real white chocolate, finely chopped

finely grated zest of 1 lemon

Chocolate Sauce (page 33), to serve

In a bowl, soak the gelatin leaves in cold water until supple.

In a small heavy-bottomed pan, bring the whipping cream to a boil with the vanilla bean and seeds from the cardamom pods. Simmer over very low heat a few minutes to infuse. Remove the vanilla bean and the cardamom, and put these to one side.

Make a ganache by pouring a little of the hot cream onto the white chocolate crumbs (page 30). Slice open the vanilla bean and scrape the seeds into the ganache; set aside.

Squeeze the excess water from the gelatin leaves, drop into the remaining hot cream, and stir until completely dissolved. Stir in the saffron and leave to steep 1 to 2 minutes; set aside to cool.

Fold the gelatin mixture into the cooled ganache, sprinkling in the lemon zest as you do. Pour the mixture into 6 small timbales, clean yogurt pots, or teacups, and chill at least 2 hours.

To serve, unmold straight from the refrigerator, with the help of a quick dip in very hot water if necessary. Serve accompanied with chocolate sauce.

mayfield muddle

This is my version of the traditional pudding "Eton Mess." Mayfield is the convent school where I was "incarcerated" for the "best years of my life." I hated that school with a passion. There were happy moments, of course, many involving chocolate. I made good friends there and found other kindred spirits who were happy to join in any subversive activities, like breaking into the domestic-science building and making chocolate crêpes.

The foundress of the convent was an American named Cornelia Connelly (referred to irreverently by the girls as "Corny Con"). She was married with five children, but she and her husband had both taken holy orders. In 1846, she was sent from Rome by Pope Gregory XVI to Derby, in England, where she founded her first convent. The story went that one of the lowly nuns from the kitchen came on bended knee to the mother foundress, begging for a farthing to buy some cloves for the apple pie. Corny Con is

reputed to have laughed and said, "No—leave it to me." She then ordered a hundred-weight of cloves, which were still being used when I was at school during the 1970s. The apple pies were certainly riddled with cloves, and, as they are an expensive spice, I suspect there must have been some truth in the tale.

This is a pretty wicked dessert, but, in fact, it doesn't contain too much fat (apart from the cream and nuts) and has loads of fresh fruit.

serves 6 to 8

7 ounces real dark chocolate

7 ounces boiling water

2 or 3 soft, but not too ripe, mangoes

6 passion fruit

1 cup heavy cream, whipped to stiff
  peaks

1 cup plain yogurt

for the meringue

³/₄ cup confectioners' sugar

4 large egg whites

4¹/₂ tablespoons unsweetened cocoa
  powder, plus more for sprinkling

1 cup finely ground blanched almonds

oil for greasing

Make the meringue: Heat the oven to 225°F and line a cookie sheet with baking parchment. (You can buy reuseable silicone sheets.) Whisk a spoonful of sugar into the egg whites and start to beat. When they start to inflate, add the remaining sugar, bit by bit, until smooth, glossy, and standing in soft peaks. Stir in the cocoa and almonds. Spread into a rough sheet or pipe into nests on the cookie sheet. Bake 4 hours, until dry and crisp. (This quantity makes almost double what you need, but this meringue will keep for a long time, so it can be made in advance and stored in an airtight container.)

While the meringue is baking, make a water ganache with the chocolate and boiling water as described on page 32; leave to cool for a couple of hours at least until thick.

Break about half the meringue into bite-size pieces. Cube the mango flesh. Cut the passion fruit in half and squeeze into the same bowl. Mix together the cream and yogurt.

In large glasses, layer the meringue, chocolate, fruit mixture and the yogurt and cream. Dust with unsweetened cocoa powder and serve.

pears with vanilla ice cream and spicy chocolate sauce

I have known Hannah as long as I can remember. My father, Tony, and Hannah's mother, Margaret, used to do "fire watching" from the rooftop of Manchester University at the end of the Second World War, and the two families have remained close friends ever since. Recently Hannah's father, Peter, "came out" as having been a spy during the war. He is now allowed to talk about his experiences, because he has been released from his sworn secrecy after fifty years. He worked for MI6 (British Intelligence Services), sending coded messages back to the UK from Addis Ababa, Izmir, and Istanbul. This is Hannah's recipe, passed down from Margaret, who got it from Elizabeth David–and, as recipes do, it has evolved along the way.

serves 4 to 6

for version 1 (the tame one)

- 4 to 6 Williams pears
- pared zest and juice of 1 lemon
- ½ cup sugar
- ½ bottle of good dry white wine
- 1 vanilla bean
- 6 whole green cardamom pods

for version 2 (the spicy one)

- 4 to 6 Conference pears
- pared zest and juice of 1 lemon
- ½ cup sugar
- bottle of good full-bodied red wine
- 1 whole red chili pepper
- piece of cinnamon
- 5 or 6 cloves
- 2 or 3 star anise
- 1 or 2 cardamom pods

to serve

- Chocolate Sauce (page 33)
- good-quality vanilla ice cream

Peel the pears, but leave them whole with the stems intact, Cover the pears with lemon juice. In a heavy-bottomed pan, dissolve the sugar in the wine and add the lemon zest, vanilla, and cardamom, or chili and other spices. Add the pears and poach until really tender. (You might have to weight them with a heatproof plate to keep them submerged.) Test the pears with a sharp knife, as the cooking time can vary from 15 minutes to an hour, depending on their ripeness and variety. When you remove the pears from the liquid, boil it until a syrupy liquid forms. Serve the pears warm or cold, with the syrup, chocolate sauce, and vanilla ice cream.

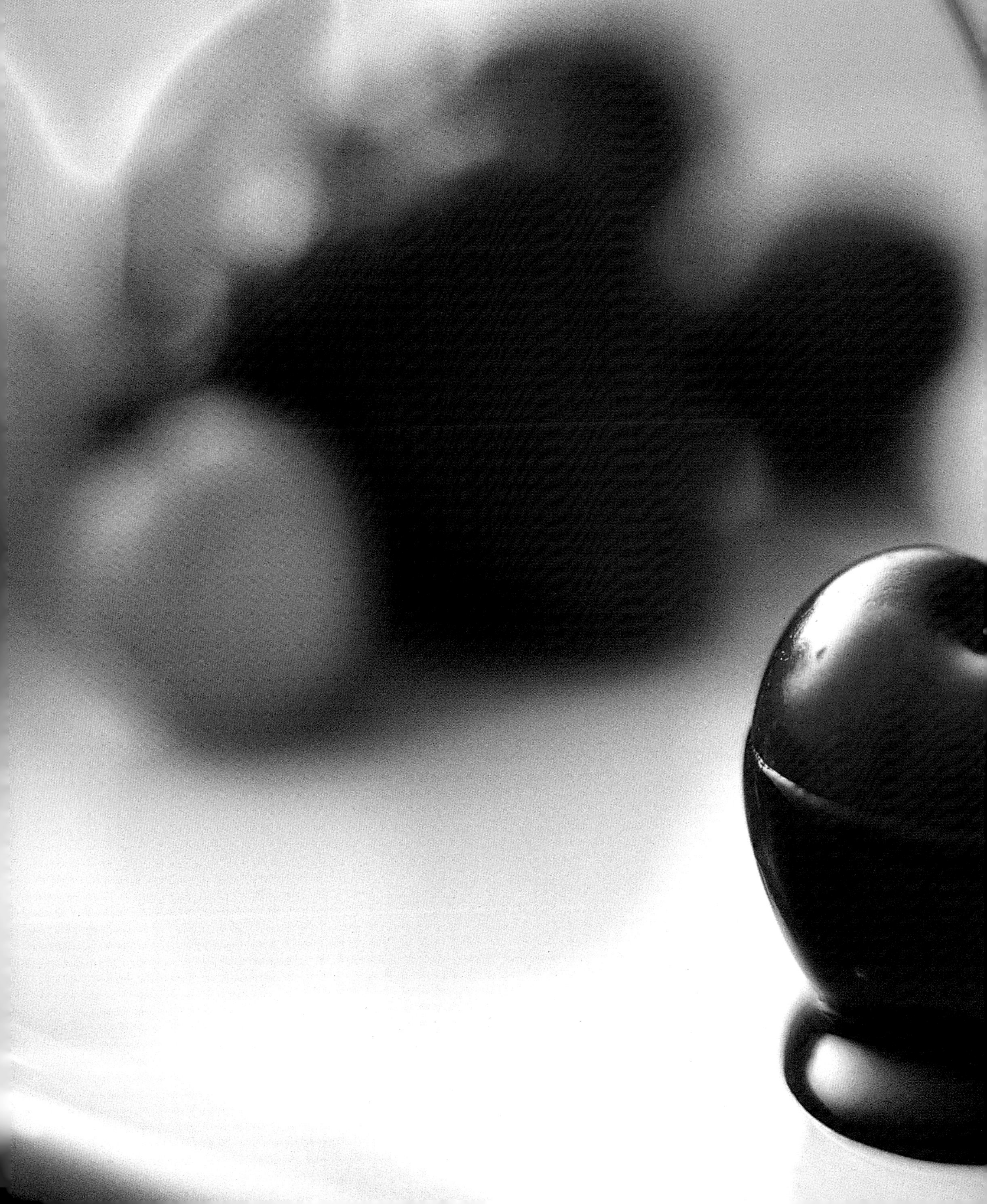

chocolate fondue

This is a simple but effective party piece. Chunks of bread or fruit of your choice can be dipped into the fondue. Ripe Williams pears, strawberries, fresh pineapple chunks, pieces of banana, nuts, and brioche all work well. If you have a fondue set, use it; otherwise, a pan or bowl does nicely.

serves 6 to 8

7 ounces real dark chocolate

$3/4$ cup whipping cream

2 tablespoons milk

1 loaf of soft country bread, French baguette, and/or brioche, torn into pieces

$1\frac{1}{4}$ pounds mixed fruits of choice (see above)

$2/3$ cup mixed shelled nuts (walnuts, Brazils, pecans)

3 to 4 ounces marshmallows

Make a ganache with the chocolate, cream, and milk as described on page 30. (The ganache can be prepared in advance and reheated patiently in the top of a double boiler, or with extreme caution over the lowest heat possible—it would be a shame to burn it.) Using fondue forks or satay sticks, simply dunk the pieces of bread, fruit, nuts, or marshmallows into the mixture— then devour.

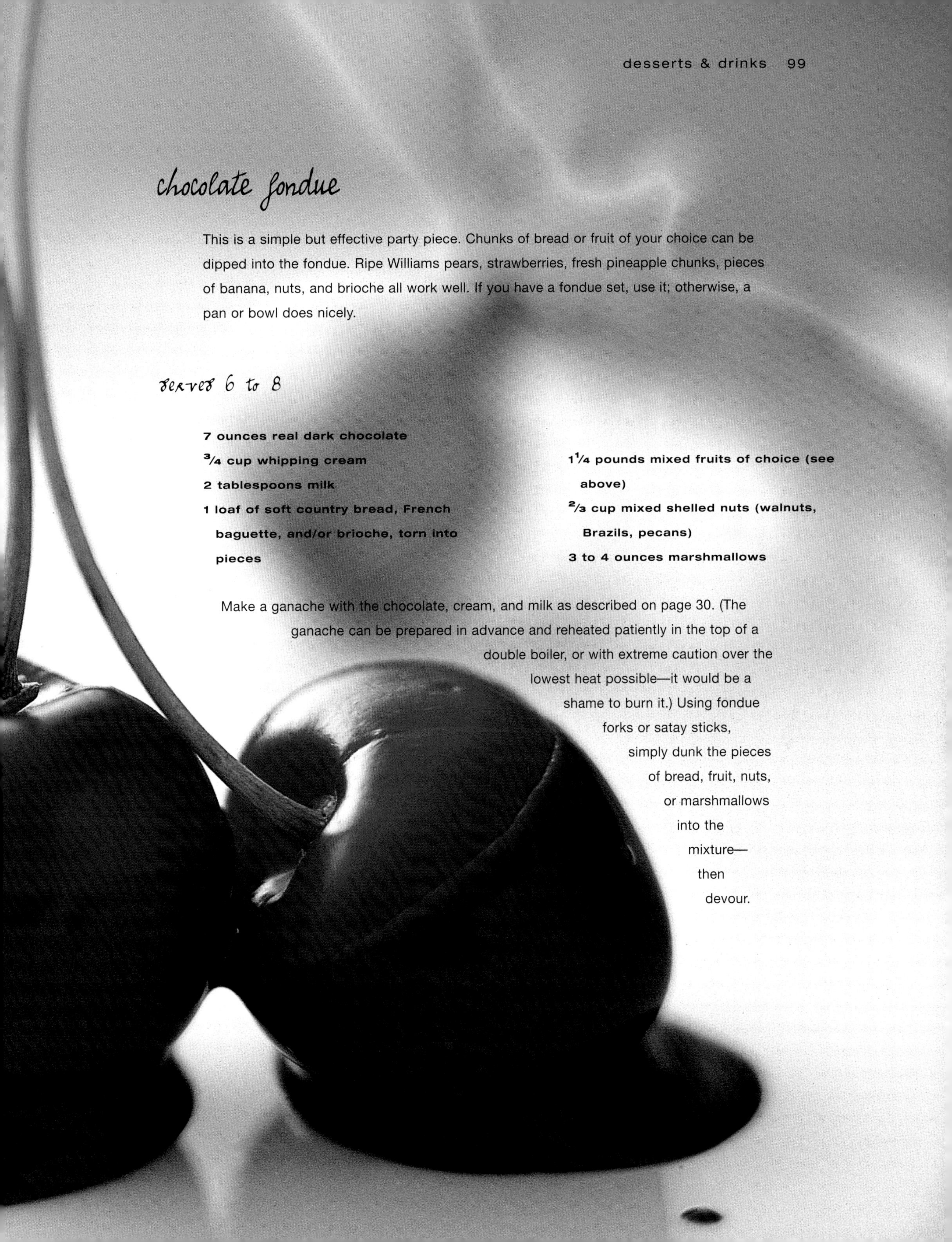

chocolate bombe filled with white chocolate risotto

This rice pudding is really a sweet risotto, but using the Middle Eastern repertoire of spices. I love this combination of flavors so much–perhaps because I was born in Teheran?

serves 8

7 ounces real dark chocolate

2 tablespoons butter

seeds from 10 green cardamom pods

2 cups risotto rice

freshly grated nutmeg

½ teaspoon real saffron strands

about 1¼ quarts milk

7 ounces real white chocolate, chopped

4 tablespoons rose water (I use Lebanese or Persian)

grappa (optional)

First prepare the bombe shell(s): Temper the dark chocolate as described on pages 40–42. Pour into a 5-cup pudding basin, a heatproof bowl, or eight ⅔-cup individual molds, and tip out the excess. This is the same process as molding the tree (page 46). You need to do this twice to get a reasonably thick layer, allowing the chocolate just to set between layers. If you are making the one large mold, then you might have some chocolate left over. (I'm sure you'll find a use for it.) Leave to cool 15 minutes, then refrigerate 30 minutes to make firm.

Make the risotto: Melt the butter in a heavy-bottomed pan over low heat. Slowly stir in the cardamom seeds and rice, taking care not to let the butter brown. Grate a good piece of nutmeg; add this and the saffron to the milk in another pan and warm slowly until almost boiling. Add a ladleful of the hot milk to the rice and stir it in. Keep stirring so the rice does not stick or become lumpy, adding more ladlefuls as it is absorbed, 20 minutes or so: The rice should be tender but still have some bite, and there should be plenty of the milky sauce. Add the white chocolate (as you would the butter and cheese to a savory risotto), together with the rose water and a slug of grappa, if you like. Stir in.

Either leave to cool and serve upside-down in the bombe case(s) or let the risotto cool a little and, when everyone is ready with bowls and spoons, pour the warm pudding into the unmolded case(s) and invert onto plates: The case(s) will melt fairy rapidly and surround the pudding in a veil of dark chocolate.

classic chocolate mousse

I first tried this recipe under the auspices of Thierry Dumouchel, the chocolate chef who worked with the Chocolate Society, in London, in its early days. It is his mother's recipe, made and enjoyed over many years. For me it was a revelation because it is so simple, with consistent results every time. It's soft, smooth chocolate mousse based on the ganache principle.

serves 8

9 ounces real dark chocolate, broken into pieces

4 tablespoons unsalted butter (½ stick), softened

9 very fresh large egg whites, plus 6 large egg yolks

heaping ½ cup super-fine sugar

Place the broken chocolate in a heatproof bowl. Melt the chocolate in an oven at very low heat, 175° to 225°F: It should melt in about 5 minutes—keep checking it with a fork. When chocolate is melted, take the bowl out of the oven and beat with the butter in a large bowl until smooth and light.

Using an electric beater, whisk the egg whites until frothy. Add 1 tablespoon sugar and continue beating slowly. When the egg whites are stiff, slowly "shake" in the remaining sugar and continue beating slowly: If you are too quick, the eggs will liquefy. Beat the meringue to make it strong and elastic, then mix in the egg yolks.

Stir half the egg mixture into the chocolate and butter mixture. Fold in the remaining egg with a large wooden spoon, working in from the outside, slowly and calmly. You need not worry about the mousse setting while you work, because the butter keeps it soft.

Pour into a large soufflé dish or 8 individual ramekins and refrigerate until set, at least 2 hours or overnight.

semifreddo

In fact, this is much the same as the recipe as I have used for my version of the River Café Chocolate Nemesis on page 87! The methods of cooking and serving it, however, result in a very different pudding, which I think should be eaten hot.

serves 6 to 8

1 cup sifted confectioners' sugar

4 very fresh large eggs, separated

pinch of salt

⅔ cup butter (1¼ sticks)

9 ounces real dark chocolate, chopped into small pieces

vanilla ice cream, to serve

Put 5 tablespoons water and half the sugar in a small pan and warm slowly, until the sugar dissolves. While this is happening, beat the egg whites with a pinch of salt and the rest of the sugar, until the consistency of a soft meringue forms.

Now stir the butter and chocolate into the syrup, and continue stirring until a smooth, melted consistency is achieved. Beat in the egg yolks, then fold in the whites bit by bit. Spoon the mixture into flexible ovenproof molds and freeze until solid, at least 2 hours or overnight.

When the mixture is frozen, heat your oven to its hottest possible setting. Put the frozen mixture into the oven and bake 5 minutes. Check to see how it's doing—if it looks well baked on the edges but not in the middle, it is just right!

You can serve immediately with vanilla ice cream or refreeze and serve frozen—if you can resist the temptation to devour it immediately.

dark chocolate and cherry "creme brulee"

Crème brûlée is one of the all-time greats in the dessert repertoire. Sometimes the choice between a chocolate pudding and a crème brûlée can mean an agonizing decision. There's no contest here! This version, devised to incorporate chocolate, is also so much easier to make than a classic crème brûlée.

serves 8

1¼ pounds very dark cherries, preferably Morello if available, pitted
finely grated zest of 1 lemon

2¼ cups crème fraîche
7 ounces real dark chocolate, finely chopped
about 1¼ cups superfine sugar

Put the pitted cherries in the bottom of 8 small ramekins and sprinkle with the lemon zest.

Bring the crème fraîche to a boil, and make a ganache with the cream and chocolate as described on page 30. Pour the ganache mixture over the cherries, and chill at least 2 hours.

Heat the sugar with 6 tablespoons water in a pan until you have a bubbling caramel mixture. Let settle briefly, then spoon carefully over the chilled pots of cherry and ganache: It should set instantly, as soon as it comes into contact with the cold mixture.

These are best served immediately.

light chocolate mousse

serves 4 to 6

1³/₄ cups whipping cream
9 ounces real dark chocolate, finely chopped

Prepare a ganache with 1 cup plus 2 tablespoons of the whipping cream and the chocolate as described on page 30. Leave the mixture to cool to about 96°F (approximately body temperature, if you don't have a thermometer).

Whip the remaining cream until it stands in soft peaks and almost doubles in volume. Using a balloon whisk, mix the whipped cream very quickly into the ganache: The result should be a semi-liquid ganache. (If not, the ganache was too cold, so return it briefly to the bain-marie.) Pour into 4 or 5 ramekins, and chill for several hours before serving.

marquise au chocolat

The marquise is a classic chocolate dessert. This version uses the Light Chocolate Mousse as its center, but there is much scope for experimentation. You might try the ganache version using water and tea or coffee (page 32) but no cream.

Serves 10 to 12

slug of very good rum (*rhum agricole* from Martinique) or some strong booze of your choice

1 mug of strong, cold espresso coffee
at least 30 boudoir chocolate cookies
1 quantity Light Chocolate Mousse (see above)
custard sauce or vanilla ice cream, to serve

Butter a 1½-quart bread pan and line it with wax paper. Mix the alcohol into the coffee. Dip the cookies into the boozy coffee until they are well soaked and use to line the pan, leaving the ends open. Pour in the mousse, cover with a layer of the dipped cookies, and leave to chill overnight.

Invert to unmold (first giving it a quick dip in warm water, if necessary) and cut into slices. Float the slices on a layer of chilled custard sauce or melted vanilla ice cream to serve.

dairy- and wheat-free chocolate roulade

For some reason I seem to be surrounded by people with special dietary requirements, so I dreamed up this basic dessert. If you don't have any problems with dairy produce and want to add a layer of whipped cream, go ahead. Give yourself free rein to experiment with the ganache; you can make it with water, tea, or coffee (page 32), and add cardamom, orange-flower water, a drop of essential oil, some bits of fruit or some booze. Using a water, tea, or coffee ganache also makes this dessert very low in fat.

serves 8

for the ganache

7 ounces real dark chocolate

7 ounces liquid of your choice (see above)

for the génoise sponge

4½ tablespoons unsweetened cocoa powder, plus more to dust

1 cup sifted confectioners' sugar

4 large eggs, separated

1 cup finely ground blanched almonds, plus more to dust

Make the ganache as described on page 32. Set to cool and then chill for about 2 hours.

To make the roulade: Heat the oven to 350°F. Sift the cocoa and sugar together and beat with the egg whites to make a soft-peak meringue. Fold in the almonds, followed by the egg yolks: Keep as much air in the batter as you can. Spread on a silicone-coated baking sheet on a large 14x17.5-inch jellyroll pan. Bake 10 to 15 minutes; leave to cool on a wire rack.

Turn out onto a piece of wax paper dusted with ground almonds. Spread the ganache over the cake and roll up like a jellyroll. Dust with cocoa powder and more ground almonds.

paul de Gondt's chocolate roulade

serves 8

for the chocolate génoise

½ cup 00 (Italian doppio zero) flour

4½ tablespoons unsweetened cocoa
powder, plus more to serve

4 large eggs, separated

½ cup sugar

pinch of salt

for the filling

Coffee, Tea, or Water Ganache (pages 30
to 32)

soft berries, crème fraîche, etc.

to serve

confectioners' sugar

Heat the oven to 400°F and line a 12x16-inch jellyroll pan with wax paper. Sift the flour
and cocoa powder together. Beat the egg whites with the salt and sugar until they attain a
meringue consistency. Beat in the egg yolks, then fold in the flour and cocoa slowly, to
keep as much air in the batter as possible. Spoon the batter into the prepared pan and
smooth the surface. Bake 12 minutes or until baked through (the tip of a knife inserted
into it will come out dry). It must not be overcooked or it will become too dry.

When the cake is cool, turn it out of the tray and remove the lining paper. Spread the
ganache over it, followed by your chosen remaining filling. Roll it up like a jellyroll and
dust with cocoa powder and confectioners' sugar.

orange and geranium pots

A couple of years ago I went to Seville for the first time in January. It was very cold and crisp, with glorious blue skies. I suppose I should have expected to see oranges, but I was bowled over by the number of orange trees in fruit on all the streets. I was being even more dense when I pondered why no one scrumped these ripe oranges. The penny dropped when we picked one and tasted it—it was too bitter to eat, but just right for marmalade. On the last morning of our stay, the Christmas lights were being taken down, so there were hundreds of windfalls lying all over the street. I could not resist the opportunity to tidy a couple of pounds into a bag and take them back to London to make marmalade. Choose your favorite oranges—they could be very tart blood oranges, or even one Seville orange mixed with some sweet oranges.

This recipe can be also be made with cream (see Chocolate Tea Pots, page 113). If you want to take a risk and make a really extreme pudding, try this one—it's a bit of a dare!

serves 6

7 ounces real dark chocolate

7 ounces freshly squeezed orange juice (oranges vary in juiciness, so it is difficult to specify a number)

about 1 cup sifted confectioners' sugar, to taste, if necessary (depending on the sweetness of the oranges)

1 drop of pure geranium essential oil

1 teaspoon orange-flower water

Finely chop the chocolate and put it into a heatproof bowl. Scald the orange juice by heating it in a small pan until boiling. Add sugar if necessary at this stage. Add the geranium oil to the hot juice. (Be careful when measuring the oil; some bottles let just one drop be dispensed, while others are not so predictable. It's probably worth dropping the oil onto a spoon, just in case.)

Make a ganache by pouring the boiling juice, bit by bit, onto the chopped chocolate (page 30). When you have blended in all the juice, add the orange-flower water to the ganache. Pour into small coffeecups, glasses, or ramekins, and chill at least 2 hours.

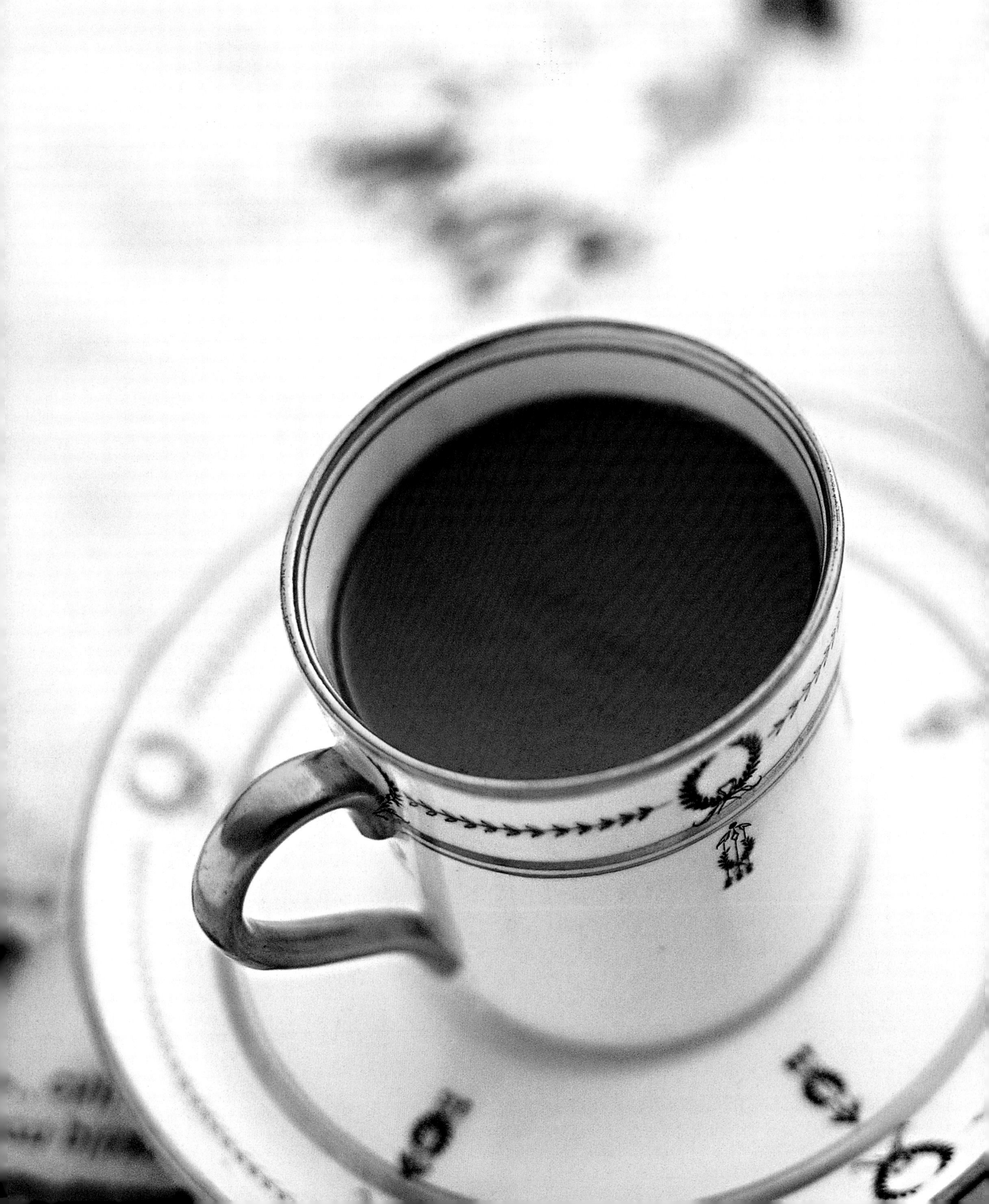

chocolate tea pots

This is one of the simplest and most delicious chocolate pudding recipes I have ever made. The scalded cream cooks the chocolate, and the tea adds a delicate perfume. The texture is sublime, and the pudding is one of the simplest forms of ganache.

serves 8

4 ounces real dark chocolate	1 tablespoon best-quality Earl Grey tea
1¾ cups light cream	1 teaspoon orange-flower water

Finely chop the chocolate and put it into a large, heatproof bowl. Scald the cream by bringing it to a boil. Add the tea and leave to stand 2 minutes; strain.

Pour the cream, bit by bit, onto the chocolate. Use a rubber spatula to stir it in, making a smooth emulsion. (If the cream gets too cool to melt the chocolate, you might have to heat it again slowly.) Add the orange-flower water.

Pour into small coffeecups, glasses, or ramekins, and chill at least 2 hours.

chocolat a l'ancienne (old-fashioned hot chocolate)

The secret recipe of Rosa Cannabich, a contemporary of Mozart, this is a wonderfully silky drink that I first tasted at a performance of "Mozart au Chocolat." It was served to the "Court" audience in the inner sanctum during a performance at the ICA gallery in London. The staging was such that a set was built with windows, and some of the seats for the audience were in that inner chamber, while the poor, miserable "rabble" outside could only look through the windows and did not get to taste the chocolate. Mozart is reputed to have drunk this hot chocolate at Mannheim in 1778. Although this recipe seems to break all the cardinal rules about heating chocolate and adding liquid, it does work and is almost a meal in itself!

serves 4

6 ounces real dark chocolate

3½ tablespoons crème fraîche

pinch of salt

2¼ cups milk

1 tablespoon superfine sugar (optional)

2 tablespoons dark rum

3½ tablespoons cold espresso coffee

To make the grated chocolate decoration, put the chocolate in the freezer for 2 hours to harden. Grate about ¾ ounce with a sharp knife or a potato peeler.

Beat the crème fraîche with an electric mixer, until stiff but not butter! Chill until you are ready to serve the chocolate.

Finely chop the remaining chocolate and place in a saucepan with the salt and 3½ tablespoons water. Melt over low heat, stirring constantly; take great care that it does not burn or the flavor will be ruined. When the chocolate is smooth and shiny, stir in the milk and then the sugar, if using. Bring to a boil, then simmer 5 minutes: Be very careful, because the chocolate bubbles up and thickens rapidly. Stir in the rum and coffee, and boil 2 minutes longer. Beat the chocolate with a whisk to lighten.

When ready to serve, add a spoonful of the whipped crème fraîche and top with the grated chocolate. In the summer, this is delicious served chilled.

chocolate vodka or gin martinis

Noilly Prat dry white vermouth

lots of ice cubes

crushed ice and/or strips of

   lemon peel (optional)

for the chocolate vodka or gin

1 bottle (700 ml) of vodka or gin

5 ounces real dark chocolate, grated or

   pulverized

Make the Chocolate Vodka or Gin, according to your preference, by melting the chocolate (page 32) and pouring it into the bottle (you might have to drink a little to make some room). Reseal and shake vigorously.

To make the chocolate martinis, in a cocktail shaker, mix 2 parts vermouth to 1 part chocolate-flavored vodka or gin, with lots of ice.

Shake or stir, according to preference, and serve in chilled martini glasses, with some crushed ice or strips of lemon peel if you feel like it.

chocolate manhattans

Make Chocolate Bourbon, as in the Chocolate Martini recipe above, using bourbon instead of vodka or gin.

Shake 1 part chocolate-flavored bourbon with 2 parts red vermouth and some crushed ice. Add a cocktail cherry and serve in a straight-sided whiskey tumbler.

cookies, cakes, & breads

classic chocolate-chip biscotti

I saw these being made at a charity auction in a palazzo near Frantoia, outside Florence. I suppose it was an Italian equivalent of a church fair, with a lot more aplomb.

makes about 30

1 cup plus 2 tablespoons lightly salted butter (2¼ sticks), softened

1 cup packed light brown sugar

½ cup plus 3 tablespoons sugar

3 large eggs

3²/₃ cups 00 (Italian doppio zero) flour, sifted

2 teaspoons real vanilla essence

7 to 12 ounces real dark chocolate chips or roughly cut pieces of real dark chocolate

Heat the oven to 350°F and line a cookie sheet with a silicone baking sheet. In a large bowl, cream the butter and sugars, then beat in the eggs. Add the sifted flour, spoonful by spoonful. When all is mixed in, add the vanilla and chocolate chips or pieces of chocolate. Spoon the mixture onto the prepared cookie sheet in 2 parallel oblongs, spaced well apart to allow for spreading: You might need more than one cookie sheet.

Bake 30 minutes until just brown on the edges; remove from the oven, but do not turn the oven off yet. Leave to cool a little, then slice the oblongs across into ½-inch-thick biscotti and return to the oven. Switch off the oven and leave the biscuits in it until cool.

stolen sardinian chocolate tart

This recipe was stolen from a famous restaurant in Sardinia, which shall remain unnamed–as will the perpetrator! Made without flour or almonds, it is so good it had to be shared.

serves 10

7 ounces real dark chocolate

½ cup unsalted butter (1 stick), plus more for the tin

8 eggs, separated

¾ cup plus 2 tablespoons sugar

⅓ cup unsweetened cocoa powder

1 tiny cup of very strong expresso coffee

Melt the chocolate in a bowl in a very low oven 5 to 10 minutes (melting chocolate, page 32). Turn the oven up to 350°F and butter a 10-inch round springform cake pan. Whisk the egg whites with the sugar until soft peaks form.

Stir the butter into the melted chocolate, then add the egg yolks, cocoa powder, and coffee. When it is all smooth and a ganache consistency (page 30), fold in the egg whites, bit by bit, until all are amalgamated.

Pour the batter into the pan and smooth the surface. Bake 30 minutes, or until a knife inserted into the middle comes out clean. Leave to cool in the pan.

chocolate brownies

This is Mandy's recipe for brownies, which are fabulously fudgy. Mandy studied Italian at university in England, where she met my husband, James. She then married an Italian air steward and now lives in "la Dolce Vita" territory near Ostia Lido, outside Rome. She leads a whirlwind life as Supermum, single-handedly bringing up three children, guiding groups of Americans around Rome, and making these famous brownies!

makes about 24 pieces

1^3/$_4$ cups butter (3 sticks)

1^1/$_2$ cups unsweetened cocoa powder

6 large eggs

3^1/$_4$ cups plus 2 tablespoons superfine sugar

1^2/$_3$ cups all-purpose flour

1 tablespoon real vanilla essence

^{3}/$_4$ cup shelled fresh walnuts, roughly chopped

Heat the oven to 350°F and line an 8x12-inch baking pan, 2 inches deep, with wax paper. In a large heavy-bottomed pan, melt the butter with the cocoa. Whisk the eggs, then whisk in the sugar, followed by the flour and vanilla. Finally add the cocoa and butter, and the nuts. Pour into the pan and bake 40 to 45 minutes: Do not overbake, or you'll loose the fudginess. Cut into squares while warm and leave to cool.

vegan chocolate biscotti

It can be daunting cooking for vegans; often one thinks of tofu and seaweed and how joyless this kind of repertoire can be in the wrong hands. Vegan seems to imply sacrifice and self-denial. There are, of course, many luxurious ingredients that can be included in the vegan repertoire, and often chocolate is overlooked, which is a shame. There should never be any dairy products or animal fats in pure dark chocolate. (As I discuss on page 17, some manufacturers actually put animal fats into their real chocolate—unforgivable!) And as chocolate is so rich in vitamins and minerals, it ought to be an essential food supplement.

This is an incredibly quick and simple Tuscan recipe that I watched being baked at the same event as the classic chocolate-chip cookies. In Italy, biscotti simply means "cookies," but the Siennese ones with which we are now so familiar are, of course, usually served with a glass of *vin santo* for dipping.

makes about 35

¾ cups 00 (Italian doppio zero) flour

½ cup superfine sugar

3½ ounces real dark chocolate, chopped into pieces

⅓ cup fresh pine nuts or walnuts

small pinch of salt

½ envelope active-dry yeast

5 tablespoons mild but good-quality extra-virgin olive oil

7 tablespoons *vin santo* (available from Italian delis or a good wine store)

Heat the oven to 350°F and line 2 or 3 cookie sheets with parchment paper.

Mix all the dry ingredients in a bowl, including the yeast. Mix well, then add the oil and *vin santo* and mix them in.

Spoon walnut-size pieces of dough onto the prepared cookie sheets, leaving plenty of space between them for spreading. Bake 8 to 10 minutes until just firm.

chocolate and gingerbread men and beasts

The whole process of making these can keep the children happy for at least an hour!

makes about 12

4½ tablespoons light corn syrup

1 large egg

2⅓ cups 00 (Italian doppio zero) flour

1 teaspoon ground cinnamon

1 teaspoon ground ginger

½ teaspoon ground cardamom

1 teaspoon baking soda

1 teaspoon unsweetened cocoa powder

7 tablespoons butter

3½ ounces chopped real dark chocolate, chopped into pieces

⅔ cup light brown sugar

M&Ms and white frosting, to decorate (optional)

Heat the oven to 400°F and line several cookie sheets with parchment paper or silicone baking sheets.

Put the corn syrup in a small bowl, then beat the egg into the syrup; set aside. Sift the flour into a separate bowl, then mix in the spices, baking soda, and cocoa powder. Put this into a food processor (you can also do this in a bowl if you prefer) and add the butter. Mix together until the mixture resembles fine crumbs. Add the chocolate, sugar, and syrup-and-egg mixture, and mix until a smooth dough is formed. If the mixture looks too dry, add up to 3 teaspoons cold water.

Roll out the dough, using extra flour if needed (you shouldn't need it), to a thickness of about ¼ inch. Stamp out shapes with a cutter or cut freehand. Put on the prepared cookie sheets and bake 10 to 15 minutes, until starting to brown at the edges and smell cooked; take care not to overbake. Transfer to a wire rack to cool, then decorate with M&Ms and white frosting if you wish.

epiphany chocolate tart

The feast of the epiphany seems to be celebrated in most Latin countries, but hardly at all anywhere else. I love the idea of the ceremony to celebrate the arrival of the three kings. Although they did not bring almonds, the nuts do seem to be in all the epiphany cakes I've ever eaten—the white chocolate was my idea.

serves 8 to 10

1 quantity Chocolate Pastry (pages 130–132)

7 ounces real white chocolate

2/3 cup blanched almonds

1 cup soft white bread crumbs (I've used pita bread, as it was all I had, but it worked admirably)

1 lemon, preferably unwaxed organic

2 large eggs, separated

pinch of salt

3 tablespoons apricot jam

good handful of black cherries (with or without the pits; leave them in for more flavor, but do then warn people!)

Butter a 9-inch loose-bottomed tart pan about 1½ inches deep. Roll out the dough and use it to line the pan, or simply mold it in with the fingers; leave to rest in the refrigerator. Melt the chocolate in an ovenproof bowl in a very low oven, 5 minutes: Don't overheat!

Turn the oven up to 325°F and bake the almonds until light brown. Chop in a food processor until ground quite fine, but they don't need to be smooth; set aside half the almonds. Turn the oven up to 350°F. Add the bread to the remaining almonds in the food processor and process until well mixed. Zest the lemon and juice it (take out seeds). Beat the egg whites with a pinch of salt until they form soft peaks. Into the melted white chocolate, beat the egg yolks, followed by the lemon zest and juice, the almonds and the bread-crumb mixture. Fold in the egg whites.

Take the tart pan out of the refrigerator, and spread with apricot jam on the bottom. Dot the cherries over that, then sprinkle the remaining ground almonds over. Cover with the batter and bake 45 minutes, or until a knife inserted into the middle comes out clean and dry. Serve warm or cold.

torta - mousse al cioccolato

This is my Italian teacher's favorite cake recipe. Annelise is a great cook and a brilliant Italian teacher—we insist that we cook together regularly as part of the course. For the lesson after she had given me this recipe, I thought I'd better make it and take it along for a critique, and when I arrived I found that she, too, had made the cake, so we were able to use it as an exercise in comparatives. I'm afraid I had the advantage, as my cake was still warm and hers had been made the day before.

My ability as a linguist is somewhat limited, but I try hard not to become one of the "let-them-speak-English" brigade. I have grown to love Italy more with each visit. The Italians understand so well how to create the perfect welcome, usually involving delicious, simple fresh food in season, which I find a great inspiration. There is now a growing movement, Slow Food, set up as a protest when McDonalds opened in the Piazza di Spagna in Rome. It has saved many small artisan producers from going out of business, and it preaches the gospel that food should be enjoyed in context and at the right pace.

serves 8 to 10

2/3 cup butter (1¼ sticks), cubed, plus
   more for greasing
1/3 cup all-purpose flour, sifted, plus more
   for dusting

10 ounces real dark chocolate
5 large eggs, separated
1 cup sifted confectioners' sugar

Heat the oven to 400°F and butter and flour a round 10-inch springform cake pan, about 4 inches deep. Melt the chocolate as described on page 32. Stir the butter into the melted chocolate. In a large bowl, beat the egg yolks with half the sugar, then add the melted chocolate and the flour.

Finally, beat the egg whites with the remaining sugar until stiff, then fold them into the batter. Pour into the pan and bake 15 to 20 minutes, until the cake feels firm when touched with palm of your hand: It's very important not to overbake this cake, because it should be very moist. When you take it out of the oven it will have risen a bit like a soufflé, but then it will deflate.

raspberry and chocolate tart

I was taken for a surprise birthday lunch to the Waterside Inn, in Bray, England, when my son was a babe in arms. He should not have been there at all but had been crying all morning–we had no choice but to take him or cancel lunch. I was very nervous about the reception we would get in this very smart Michelin-starred restaurant (three stars at that time) when rolling up with an infant. In fact, he was in marvelous humor when we arrived, and we were all welcomed like long-lost friends. The Europeans definitely understand that children, however young, should be encouraged in gastronomy. I chose the raspberry and chocolate tart for pudding, and it was sublime. This is my attempt to recreate it.

serves 8 to 10

1 quantity Chocolate Pastry (pages 130–132)
1 pound raspberries
vanilla-flavored confectioners' sugar, to dust
cream, custard sauce or the best real

vanilla ice cream, to serve

for the ganache
10 ounces real dark chocolate, plus more for the crust
1¼ cups whipping cream or crème fraîche

Make the pastry dough, use it to line a tart pan, and bake blind as described on pages 130–32 for about 20 minutes, or until cooked; set aside to cool completely.

Make the ganache as described on page 30. When the pastry is cool and the ganache has cooled to a thick custard-like consistency, arrange most of the raspberries on the tart crust, keeping a good handful for serving.

You can paint the crust with a thin layer of melted/tempered (pages 40–42) chocolate if you can be bothered, but you don't need to. Pour the ganache over the raspberries and leave in the refrigerator to set at least a couple of hours.

Serve with the remaining raspberries piled on the top and dusted with vanilla-flavored confectioners' sugar. Serve with cream, custard sauce, or the best real vanilla ice cream.

pear and chocolate tart

This is an old favorite in our house. It has been through many incarnations and can be adapted to suit your mood. Sometimes I bake it for much longer than indicated below (it's better firmer if it's to be served warm), and sometimes I put a layer of Seville orange marmalade on the crust before adding the pears. This version uses a variation on the ganache theme, substituting custard sauce for cream in the ganache. The whites of the eggs are whipped and added at the end to give an even airier effect. The whole thing is much lighter than the cream-based ganache version. If you're not worried about lightly cooked eggs, you can even use this mixture unbaked. The dough can be made the day before, or a larger quantity can be prepared well in advance and frozen.

serves 8 to 10

for the chocolate pastry

2³/₄ tablespoons unsweetened cocoa powder

1 cup very fine flour, ideally 00 (Italian doppio zero), plus more for dusting the pan

pinch of salt

1/₃ cup confectioners' sugar, plus more for dusting the tart

6 tablespoons unsalted butter (³/₄ stick), roughly cubed, plus more for greasing the pan

1 large egg yolk

for the filling

2 large eggs, separated

2¹/₂ tablespoons sugar

1¹/₄ cups milk

1 vanilla bean

10 ounces real dark chocolate, finely chopped in food processor until the consistency of bread crumbs and just beginning to melt

3 large or 4 small ripe but firm pears, preferably Williams

to decorate and serve

cape gooseberries

whipping cream, crème fraîche, or vanilla ice cream

To make the pastry dough, sift the cocoa powder, flour, salt, and confectioners' sugar together. Place in a food processor with the butter and, using the metal blade, mix until fine crumbs form. Add the egg yolk and pulse gently until you have a lump of dough. Wrap in plastic wrap and chill for an hour or so.

When the dough is firm, heat the oven to 350°F and generously butter and flour the bottom and side of a round, loose-bottomed 10-inch tart pan, 1½ inches deep. Roll the dough out and then place the bottom in the pan. Don't worry if the dough breaks; it is very short and can easily be repaired. Roll out the trimmings of the dough and use to line the side, pressing the dough into the corners. The top edge of the dough can be very thin and left with a rough finish; it will have an attractive lacy look when baked. Prick all over with a fork and bake 15 minutes; set aside to cool on a wire rack.

To make the filling, first prepare a custard: Beat the egg yolks and sugar in a heatproof bowl. In a separate pan, bring the milk with the vanilla bean to a boil, then whisk the boiling milk into the egg mixture with a balloon whisk. Keep whisking until the mixture thickens. If the mixture is not hot enough to thicken, return it briefly to low heat, but be very careful or you'll end up with scrambled eggs! When you have a light custard (it doesn't need to be too thick), pour it little by little onto the chocolate to make the ganache, as described on page 30.

Peel the pears, cut them in half, and scoop out the cores and stems. Arrange the pear halves on the baked tart shell.

Whisk the egg whites in a clean bowl (you will have 2 or 3, depending on when you made the pastry—either is fine) until forming soft peaks. Beat one-quarter into the custard, then fold the remainder in gently. Pour the filling over the pears.

Bake about 30 minutes, or until risen and set to your taste. You can decide whether you want a soft filling or a firmer one, depending on how long you bake the tart; soft is best if serving cold, and a firmer set is better for serving hot.

Decorate with cape gooseberries and dust with confectioners' sugar. Serve hot or cold, with whipping cream, crème fraîche, or vanilla ice cream.

chocolate pound cake with white chocolate frosting

This is based on a classic pound cake recipe. It is a very simple cake, not too rich and suitable for making on a large scale.

serves 10

7 tablespoons butter, plus more for greasing

8 ounces real dark chocolate

1½ cups flour

1 tablespoon baking powder

1 cup packed light brown sugar

3 extra-large eggs

1 cup sour cream or crème fraîche

1 teaspoon real vanilla essence

unsweetened cocoa powder, to dust

for the white chocolate frosting

7 ounces real white chocolate

7 ounces whipping cream, crème fraîche, or sour cream

Heat the oven to 350°F and butter a large kugelhopf mold (any mold will do, but keep checking, because the baking times will vary in other molds). Melt half the chocolate as described on page 32.

Sift together the flour and baking powder, Using the metal blade in the food processor, beat the butter, sugar, eggs, crème fraîche, sifted flour mixture, and vanilla. When it is all mixed, add the melted chocolate and give it a final mix.

Pour the batter into the mold and bake 30 to 45 minutes, until a skewer inserted into the middle of the cake comes out clean; leave to cool in the mold, then unmold.

To make the white chocolate frosting, melt the white chocolate very carefully as described on page 32: Do not overheat. Beat the cream until it starts to thicken. Fold the cream into the melted chocolate as per the Ganache recipe (page 30) and chill until stiff.

Spread the frosting on the cake and dust with unsweetened cocoa powder.

sephardic chocolate and almond cake

This is a variation on Claudia Roden's recipe that has been one of our family favorites for years—another must-have for the annual family cricket match. My brother-in-law, Simon Roden, first introduced me to this cake.

serves 8 to 10

8 ounces real dark chocolate

2 tablespoons unsalted butter (¼ stick), cut into pieces, plus more for greasing

5 large eggs, separated

¾ cup plus 2 tablespoons superfine sugar

1 cup very finely ground blanched almonds

2 tablespoons milk

1 teaspoon apple vinegar

to decorate (optional)

confectioners' sugar

unsweetened cocoa powder

Melt the chocolate as described on page 32. After taking the chocolate out of the oven, turn the temperature up to 350°F and butter a 10-inch springform cake pan. Beat the butter into the melted chocolate. Whisk the egg whites with the sugar to meringue/soft peak consistency. Beat in the egg yolks and then fold in the ground almonds. Fold the egg-white mixture into the chocolate and butter, and finally add the milk and vinegar. (The vinegar stops the cake from cracking too much when it rises.)

Pour into the pan and bake 35 to 45 minutes, or until a skewer inserted into the cake comes out clean; leave the cake to cool in the pan on a wire rack.

Turn out the cake and sprinkle with confectioners' sugar and/or cocoa powder. Or, if you like, make a paper stencil of a hare, a lamb, or any other motif. First lightly dust the whole cake with cocoa powder, then lay the stencil on the cake and sift the confectioners' sugar through it. (You can use a tea strainer, if you want to be more accurate.) Lift the paper off very carefully when you are finished.

Brioche with chocolate nibs

Brioche is sometimes served toasted as an accompaniment to foie gras. Here it contains cocoa nibs, which add crunch to contrast with the other textures. Chocolate Balsamic Vinegar (page 60) could also be used if the foie gras was served with some salad leaves.

makes 1 large loaf

1 teaspoon active-dry yeast

¼ cup sugar

2 tablespoons milk, warm

2⅔ cups 00 (Italian doppio zero) flour

pinch of salt

3 eggs, lightly beaten

⅔ cup butter (1¼ sticks), softened, plus more for greasing

2 ounces cocoa nibs (page 59)

The day before, dissolve the yeast in a small bowl with 1 tablespoon of the sugar in the milk, then set aside until it starts to bubble and froth.

Meanwhile sift the flour into a large bowl, then stir in the salt. Add the yeast mixture, eggs, remaining sugar, and butter, and beat everything until well mixed. Leave the dough in a warm place 2 to 4 hours, or until doubled in size.

Push down the dough with a wooden spoon, then put it in a greased, clean bowl, cover with plastic wrap, and leave overnight in a cool place.

In the morning, butter a large kugelhopf or brioche mold. Punch down the dough and knead it briefly until all the air has been squeezed out. Knead in the cocoa nibs, then put the dough into the buttered mold and cover with plastic wrap. Leave in a warm place 3 to 4 hours, or until the dough rises to the top of the mold.

Meanwhile, heat the oven to 375°F. Bake the brioche 20 to 25 minutes, or until it is golden brown and sounds hollow when tapped on the base. (You will need to turn it out of the mold to do this.) If it is not ready, you can return it to the mold and the oven to continue baking. Turn out the brioche and leave to cool on a wire rack.

chocolate breakfast muffins or quick bread

This versatile recipe, an old family favorite from my mother-in-law, can be baked shaped either as muffins or as a loaf. No cricket tea is complete without the latter. This version has less sugar than the traditional one and no added fat. The chocolate is my addition. You do need to think ahead, however, as it needs a good night's sleep! Other than that, it is very quick to make and extremely simple. Serve the loaf cold, thinly sliced and buttered, with a cup of tea or for breakfast. Alternatively, use paper muffin cases and bake about 20 minutes for a late breakfast—eat warm!

makes 8 to 10 muffins

2/3 cup dried fruit

1/4 cup packed light brown sugar

7 ounces cold tea

butter, for greasing

1 egg

1 tablespoon rich dark Seville orange marmalade

1½ cups self-rising flour

1 teaspoon apple-pie spice

2 ounces real dark chocolate, chopped into small chunks

The day before, put the fruit, sugar, and tea in a bowl or pitcher and leave overnight.

The next day, heat the oven to 350°F and grease a 5½ x4½-inch bread pan well, or arrange 8 to 10 paper muffin wrappers on a cookie sheet. In a large mixing bowl, beat the egg with the marmalade and add the overnight mixture of tea, sugar, and fruit. Sift in the flour and spice. Add the chocolate and mix into the other ingredients.

Pour the batter into the pan or muffin wrappers and bake 1 hour for the loaf or 20 to 30 minutes for the muffins, or until the top(s) spring back when pressed. Leave to cool in the pan or wrappers 20 minutes before turning onto a wire rack to cool completely.

acknowledgments

A special thank you to Paul de Bondt. A very big thank you to: Alessandro Balestri, Roberto Bava, Michael Coe, Alan Davidson, Rose Gray, Eugenio Guarducci, Cecilia Iacobelli, Madhur Jaffrey, Tina Lambi, Monica Meschini, Claudia Roden, Ruth Rogers, Andrea Slitti, and Lydia Sodani. Francoise Dietrich, Lewis Esson, Richard Foster, Jane Suthering, Thom, Emma, Katie, and all the team. Jane O'Shea, Alison Cathie, and all at Quadrille for their unwavering support. To my team at Rococo, especially Jo and Ruth, and to all the loyal Rococo supporters. Finally to the Coady Family, including the Booths, Galtons, and Rodens, and Kati Iglai.

bibliography

John Ashton & Suzy Ashton **A Chocolate a Day**
(Keeps the Doctor away) Souvenir Press 2001

Frederic Bau **Au Coeur des Saveurs** Montagud Editores,
Barcelona 1998

Sophie and Michael Coe **The True History of Chocolate** Thames and Hudson 1996

Madhur Jaffrey **Eastern Vegetarian Cooking** Jonathan
Cape 1983; (paper) Arrow 1990

Claudia Roden **Mediterranean Cookery** BBC Books 1987

Eric Schlosser **Fast Food Nation** Houghton Mifflin 2001

suppliers

Rococo
321 Kings Road
Chelsea, London SW3 5EP
tel 020 7352 5857
www.rococochocolates.com or www.rococo.ro
Full international mail-order service
(Those trying to obtain cocoa nibs, currently supplied in
the UK only by Rococo, should call.)

The Chocolate Society
36 Elizabeth Street
London SW1W 9NZ
tel 020 7259 9222
mail-order service (UK only) 01423 322230
www.thechocolatesociety.co.uk

The author also recommends readers look for Valrhona
(www.valrhona.com), Barry Callebaut, Scharffenberger, and
Green & Blacks (www.greenandblacks.com).
The best sources for real chocolate would be good
delicatessens, supermarkets, or department stores.

www.chocolocate.com provides a list of worldwide
chocolate and equipment suppliers.

Rococo chocolates can also be found at
The Fine Cheese Co, 29-31 Walcot Street, Bath BA1 5BN
tel 01225 483407
Algerian Coffee Stores, 52 Old Compton Street, London
W1V 6PB tel 020 7437 2480
East Dulwich Deli 15–17 Lordship Lane, London SE22
8EW tel 020 8693 2525
The Conran Shop Chelsea, Michelin House, Fulham
Road, London SW3 6RD tel 020 7589 7401
The Conran Shop, 55 Marylebone High Street, London
W1U 5HS tel 020 7723 2223
The Conran Shop Paris Rive Gauche, 117 Rue du Bac,
75007 Paris tel 1 42 84 10 01

Good suppliers of chocolate molds, operating a mail-order
service, are Vantage House and Chocolate World, both at
www.vantage-house.com